Myrtle Moore

THE ORIGIN OF ALL THINGS

THE ORIGIN OF ALL THINGS

Studies in Genesis

HERSCHEL H. HOBBS

WORD BOOKS
Waco, Texas

Library of Congress catalog card number: 75–36191
Printed in the United States of America

To the late H. C. Brown, Jr.,
my former pupil and a master teacher
of preaching

CONTENTS

1

CREATION'S DAWN

Genesis 1:1–31

"In the beginning God created the heaven and the earth." Thus begins the message of the Bible. The late eminent physicist, Arthur Compton, called these words the most tremendous ever penned. They are a fitting beginning for this book of *beginnings*. So majestic in tone and all-encompassing in magnitude are they that it seems almost sacrilegious to touch them or probe their meaning. Yet they are so vital to our faith and to our understanding of God, ourselves, and our world that they call for deep and reverent consideration. If you can believe the first four words in the Bible, all else becomes both clear and credible. In the words of Caedmon, written over twelve centuries ago, we stand in awe as we view creation's dawn.

> Now must we praise the glory of Heaven's Kingdom,
> The Creator's might, and His mind the thought,
> The glorious Father's works, and how to wonders all
> He gave beginning, He, the Eternal Lord!

Other ancient people besides the Hebrews had accounts of creation. Their lengthy, complicated stories portray creation's dawn in terms of many pagan deities. A cardinal principle in literary criticism is that the shorter, simpler of two accounts of the same event is the older and more accurate. According to this principle the Genesis record is the fountainhead from which flow the others, embellished by their pagan deities. While men

9

may have wandered from the true God, they retained the kernel of truth concerning the beginning of all things as being a direct act of deity. These numerous, embellished stories do not dilute the truth of the Bible; rather they point to a common source of simple truth which is found in pure form in Genesis 1.

The Bible clearly teaches that man began by worshiping the one true God (Gen. 1; Rom. 1) and gradually drifted into the worship of many gods. For many years certain scholars held that the opposite was true, but within the past generation archeology and anthropology, working independently, have confirmed the record of the Bible. As though anticipating the views of the skeptics, in Genesis 2 the Holy Spirit led Moses to declare that the God (*Elohim*) who created is the "Lord God" (*Yahweh Elohim*), the true God, Jehovah (see Deut. 6:4–5). As we view the majestic account in Genesis 1, creation dawns in all its glorious splendor.

A Factual Account

In simplest terms Genesis 1 records the factual events of God's creative work. Obviously Moses was not present when they unfolded. But writing under the inspiration of the Holy Spirit, he told the story in such a way that no fact of his account conflicts with modern scientific conclusions as to the order and progress of the events. Moses did not propose to write a scientific treatise but to pen in language comprehended by his readers the origin of all things. The Holy Spirit was not concerned primarily with time or detailed methods but with the sublime truth that all things came into being through the creative work of God. Science is concerned with the *what;* the Bible is concerned with the *Who.* The *how* does not lend itself to dogmatics. God reveals himself through both the Bible and nature. Theories about either may conflict, but truth in both agree, for all truth is of God!

In two brief verses Moses sets the stage: "In the beginning God created the heaven and the earth. And the earth was without form, and void; and darkness was upon the face of the deep. And the Spirit of God moved upon the face of the waters" (vv. 1–2).

"In the beginning"—whenever that was—may be as broad or as narrow as the scope of man's limited knowledge. Centuries ago Archbishop James Ussher (A.D. 1581–1656) sought to arrive at the date of creation by working back from fixed dates in history. He concluded that creation occurred in 4004 B.C. His contemporary, Professor Lightfoot of Cambridge University (A.D. 1602–1675), set creation week as October 18–24, 4004 B.C. He even fixed the time of man's creation as 9:00 A.M., October 23, 4004 B.C.! Personally, apart from the lack of scientific accuracy, I have always resented this date. Had he made it one day later, it would have been on my birthday in 1907!

Quite obviously this attempt to date creation does not coincide with modern scientific discoveries. Ruins of civilizations have been found which antedate this time by many centuries. One is on safe grounds in placing Abraham's date about 2000–1900 B.C., but behind that time what Ussher regarded as generations most likely involved vast periods of time which do not submit to man's dating processes. Until the Holy Spirit began to trace God's redemptive purpose in history, beginning with Abraham, he revealed the *beginnings* which evidently involved not years but vast uncharted periods of time.

Science, using tools such as the carbon test, speaks of millions, even billions of years since creation's dawn. A recent exploration on the moon revealed orange-colored soil. One wag suggested that the astronauts had spilled some Tang, but preliminary scientific examination suggests that this substance may be as much as four and one-half billion years old. When this soil was discovered, the astronauts were looking for the "Genesis" rock.

Does such a conclusion invalidate the Bible? Not at all. The

Bible does not propose to satisfy man's curiosity; it merely tells us that all material things had a beginning. Should science prove beyond a shadow of doubt that the universe is billions of years old, it would not affect adversely the Bible record one whit. Creation took place "in the beginning"—that is as flexible as any future conclusion of research. What the Bible does is to refute the idea of the eternity of matter. Theories are a dime a dozen. They are but the tools of research which are tried, and if found faulty, are cast aside. The more that sober men of science delve into the mysteries of the universe, the less dogmatic they become. Today, responsible men of science look for a "beginning." They too are saying, "In the beginning."

The Bible is content to say, "In the beginning God created the heaven and the earth," or every material thing. Only God is eternal; all else is the result of his creative work. Nowhere does the Bible seek to prove the existence of God, but it declares that before anything was he is. Psalm 90 is attributed to Moses. In repeated eloquence he says, "Lord, thou hast been our dwelling place in all generations. Before the mountains were brought forth, or ever thou hadst formed the earth and the world, even from everlasting to everlasting, thou art God" (Ps. 90:1-2).

Someone asked a great philosopher, "You have spent your life asking questions and seeking answers. If you had but one question to ask, what would it be?" He replied, "Is the universe friendly?" His answer is found in the phrase, "In the beginning God."

No longer do those out on the spearpoint of scientific research regard the universe as a giant, impersonal machine grinding on and on. By whatever name they may call him, they see an originating and guiding Personality. Sir James Jeans said that back of the universe is a great Mind. He called it a "Mathematical Mind." When man split the atom, the building blocks of the universe, he used, not a hammer and chisel, but a mathematical formula.

Andrew M. Fairbairn in *The Philosophy of the Christian Reli-*

gion* (p. 49) says, "Whether mind may be conceived without matter, is a point that may be argued; but matter can be represented in no form which does not imply mind . . . The highest speculations concerning the ultimate cause have been expressed in the terms of intellect or the reason." He concludes (p. 55) that "we cannot conceive either Nature or its creative work otherwise than through Mind . . . To affirm the transcendence of thought is to affirm the priority of spirit, for spirit is but thought made concrete . . . and how can we better express this thought in its highest concrete form than by the ancient name of God?"

The universe is friendly to those who would be its friend. For behind it, indwelling it, but above and beyond it, is God. And God is love (1 John 4:8)!

In Genesis 1:2 the writer moves from the general to the specific. Having stated that God created the universe as a whole, he focuses upon the earth. Though the earth is one of the lesser planets in size, it is the arena of God's activity in both his loving care and his redemptive purpose. Thus far, space probing has failed to find on other heavenly bodies conditions for life as we know it. I find myself in agreement with the astronaut's view. Hurtling back to earth after a moon exploration, he described earth's beauty in contrast to the barren moon: "God did something special on the earth." Astronaut Ronald Evans, commander of the *Apollo 17* mission, says that the significance of the space flights is not so much material as it is aesthetic, emotional, and philosophical. Seeing planet Earth from a distance makes it clear, he said, that "it's too beautiful and perfect for it to have happened by accident, that there is someone greater than us all."

By anticipation, under the guidance of the Holy Spirit, Moses turns his attention to details as to how God created the earth. "And the earth was without form, and void; and darkness was upon the face of the deep" (v. 2).

Some interpreters see a catastrophic gap between verses 1 and

---

* Full information about books referred to in the text may be found in the Bibliography at the end of this volume.

2. They hold that God created the earth in perfection, and then sent a judgment upon it when certain rebellious angels were cast out of heaven into the earth. This view is related to Isaiah 45:18: "He created it not in vain." The same Hebrew word is translated "in vain" in Isaiah and "without form" in Genesis 1:2. It is also pointed out that the Greek translation of the Old Testament uses the verb *to become* in Genesis 1:2, implying that the earth *became* what it was not in the beginning.

However, to me this seems a forced interpretation. To begin with, this Greek verb may also be translated "came into being." Also, Isaiah 45:18 refers to God's ultimate purpose in creation. I agree with Basil F. C. Atkinson (p. 12). Speaking about fixing our attention upon the earth, he says, "It is the first step in a process of continuous narrowing. The process of God becomes concentrated, as we read the Bible, upon a single nation, then upon a single family in it, and finally upon a lonely sublime figure hanging in anguish on Calvary's cross. There the purpose widens again step by step, till it finally embraces a whole creation, a new heaven and a new earth."

To say that the earth was "without form and void" could mean that it was an *empty nothingness*. But since it was the "earth," this is hardly the case. Rather it may mean that the earth mass was shapeless and without vegetable or animal life. And since there was as yet no light to penetrate the vapor about the earth (see v. 3), "darkness was upon the face of the deep," or the water that enveloped the earth. The figure is that of an unfinished, not a ruined, creation.

Science sees the origin of the earth as a molten, shapeless mass. As this mass spun about on its axis, there were upheavals as it assumed form. In the cooling process, vapor or water formed to cover it. The ancients used terms which accurately describe this process: Hebrew *aretz*, "to break in pieces"; Greek *chthōn*, "to bind to itself," or gravity; Latin *terra*, "to wear away," or erosion. These words suggest various phases of how this empty, shapeless mass took on the form known as the earth.

"And the Spirit of God moved upon the face of the waters" (v. 2). The third person of the Trinity is introduced into the account. The Spirit of God is God's Spirit sent forth to do his work and is always associated with power. He is called both the "Spirit of God" and the "Spirit of Christ." In effect, here he expresses the triune God. The New Testament repeatedly states that Christ was the intermediate agent in the creative process.

G. Henton Davies (p. 125) sees this figure as a mighty hurricane that moved the water surrounding the shapeless mass. To be sure, the Hebrew word for *Spirit* means also wind or breath, but the word rendered *moved* hardly allows this meaning. Basically it means "to brood" (it is translated "fluttereth" in Deut. 32:11). So it seems that the Spirit was brooding over the chaotic mass to bring it from a *chaos* to a *cosmos*. In this manner God prepared the earth for his further creative work.

Genesis 1:3-26 records a series of words spoken by God, each resulting in certain conditions obtaining upon the earth. "And God said" introduces each new phase of his creative work. Psalm 33:6 says, "By the word of the Lord were the heavens made; and all the host of them by the breath of his mouth."

At this point two things concern us—the time element and the order of creation. We are familiar with the *six days* of God's creative work and his *seventh day* of rest. The Hebrew word for *day* (*yom*), like the English word, was used variously. It could mean the period between dawn and dusk (Gen. 1:5, 14), a twenty-four-hour period (Gen. 8:3–14), a signal event in history (Isa. 13:6; Jer. 46:10; Ezek. 30:3), a generation (Num. 14:34), an era in history (2 Kings 19:3; Ps. 20:1; Hab. 3:16), or a period of indefinite time, an age (Isa. 65:2). These varied uses should provide caution in reckoning the length of *day* in Genesis 1.

Obviously if we hold to six twenty-four-hour days, there is conflict between the Bible and the suggested periods of science comprising millions or billions of years. However, noting the various uses of *day* we are not forced to confine the creative work to six days of twenty-four hours each. The sun and moon are not mentioned until the fourth day. The *days* of creation may be of twenty-four-hour length or indefinite periods of time. It is not a question as to how much time God needed, but how much he used. He could have done it all in an atomic fraction of a second, or he could have used millions or billions of years. Time is no object with God (2 Pet. 3:8).

Should scientists prove beyond doubt that the time involved billions of years, it would not affect the accuracy of Genesis 1. God created "in the beginning"—whenever that was—and he used *days* of whatever length he willed. The Holy Spirit led Moses to use language that can fit any time schedule. We must not try to tell God how much time he used. God did it, and we can leave the time element with him. The Holy Spirit was not concerned with time or detailed methods but with the sublime truth that all things come into being through the creative work of God.

When we turn to the *order* of creation, once again there need be no conflict between the Bible and science. Both agree as to the primacy of water upon or about the earth. Light appeared on the *first day* of creation. The fact that *day* is followed by *night* suggests that this light came from another heavenly body (see vv. 14–18). Some scientists call this "cosmic light." One theologian sees the first-day light as the invasion of God into the earth pattern, but since God is omnipresent, this is hardly necessary.

The *second day* was the occasion for the formation of the "firmament," or limitless expanse, as God divided earth water from atmospheric water. This period coincides with the pre-Paleozoic age of science. Science estimates the weight of atmospheric water at 54,460,000,000,000 tons. The weight of water is 773 times that of air. Which speaks of God's power as seen daily in evaporation. Using different language the Bible and science express the same truth for this period in creation.

On the *third day* dry land, seas, and vegetation appeared. Note Moses' use of *seas*. He knew of the Mediterranean and Red Seas, but we now speak of seven seas. *Seas* was used by divine revelation, not human reason. Mention has already been made of the ancient words for *earth*. The Hebrew word (*aretz*), which antedates the others, suggests convulsions or earthquakes which caused the earth's surface to rise in certain areas. This brought about the breaking up or crumbling of the planet to form mountains, valleys, and seas (*terra*). By gravity, water adhered to the earth (*chthōn*). Such a statement might have been lifted from a textbook in geology, which shows again the general harmony between the Scriptures and science.

Plant life also emerged on the *third day*. Note the two varieties: that with seed in the plant; that with seed in its fruit. The emphasis is upon the method of reproduction, each "after its kind." This also is affirmed by botany.

On the *fourth day* the sun, moon, and stars appear. They not only divide day from night, but also determine the "signs" or compass points, as well as seasons and years. All of these are in agreement with the most up-to-date scientific knowledge. The terminology may differ, but the facts are the same.

As I watch television on a certain station, every hour on the hour a sharp sound is heard. Usually I glance at my watch to see if it is correct. This sound is made by light rays from a certain star, and it serves to declare the exactness of time. The heavenly bodies not only determine times, days, and seasons, but they enable earth time to be fixed with precision.

So precise are these schedules that astronomers can predict exactly where a given planet will be at any future time. It requires more faith to believe that this is by accident than to accept the fact that God directs the paths of the planets.

In 1965 the Southern Baptist Radio and Television Commission, Fort Worth, Texas, broke ground for a new building. It was my privilege to be the speaker for the occasion. Through special arrangement, ground was broken by dynamite detonated by an impulse from a certain star. It had to be in an exact position to do this. Scientists monitoring the star were to tell us the exact second when this would be the case. Right in the middle of my speech I was told to pause for a moment. Exactly on schedule the dynamite exploded, after which I finished my message. Truly through scientific exactness "the heavens declare the glory of God; and the firmament sheweth his handywork" (Ps. 19:1).

However, at this point, some pose a problem between science and the Bible. They insist that the order in placing plant life before the sun is wrong, since the sun's rays are necessary for plant life. But the Bible does not say that these heavenly bodies were *created* on the fourth day. The sun and moon were *made* (*asah,* not *bara,* "to create," v. 1). Some interpreters see them as made out of previously created matter. However, there is another possible meaning which clears up the problem. *Asah* may mean to release from restraint. If this be true here, these heavenly bodies were created as in verse 1. The sun was released from restraint on the fourth day in that its rays penetrated the mist which surrounded the earth. But its life-giving rays had been bombarding the earth all the while, making not only light and darkness (vv. 3–5) but also making possible plant life. You can get a sunburn on a cloudy day; whether or not you see the sun, its rays are penetrating the clouds.

According to astronomers the planet Jupiter is still enveloped in such a mist, so that insofar as science knows the direct rays of the sun do not penetrate to its surface. Jupiter, therefore, is called "the fourth-day planet," giving scientific recognition to Genesis 1:16.

On the *fifth* day marine and bird life appeared. Science affirms that life on earth first appeared in water. The mention of bird life along with marine life is significant, since both are similar in nature. Birds and fish have similar bodily structures. Both are oval to enable them to move through their natural habitat. They are suspended in air and water respectively. Birds have wings and fish fins to propel them through their natural habitats. Their bodies are protected by feathers (birds) and scales (fish). Both have hollow bones to give them buoyancy. Both have oval blood corpuscles and are migratory.

The fact that the Bible and science agree that life began in water does not mean that the Bible supports the theory that this water life gradually evolved into land creatures. To the contrary, the Bible record clearly separates life into its various categories as direct creations of God. To date, science has produced no *facts* which refute this. We should be careful not to make the Bible say more than it says, but we should also beware of unproved *theories* which would make the Bible say less than it actually does.

The *sixth* day of creation tells of the creation of life on land. This included cattle, domesticated animals which feed upon herbs, beasts or wild animals which feed upon meat, reptiles and insects, and finally man. Science agrees with this order. Each phase of this life is to reproduce after its "kind." There might be development within species, but the Bible gives no hint that one would ever become another. (See chapter 2 for a more detailed treatment of man.)

Having finished his creative work, God *rested* on the *seventh day*. This does not mean that he was tired but that he ceased his creative work. No evidence exists that any other natural creation has been done. God is now busy re-creating men and redeeming a fallen nature (see John 5:17; 2 Cor. 5:17). This rest on the seventh *day* implies a period of indefinite length, which tends to confirm the use of the six days as indefinite periods of time, perhaps of varying lengths. It is well to recall once again that it is not a matter primarily of the time involved, but that the universe and all that is in it is a creation of God and not an accident of blind chance.

A Theological Explanation

There is no basis for conflict between science and the biblical account of creation; yet Moses was not writing a scientific treatise. The Bible is a book of religion. It tells about God and his eternal purpose in dealing with the universe and man, with the primary emphasis upon man. The earth is the scene both of man's sin and the drama of divine redemption. In this early account of the *beginnings,* Moses was primarily concerned with man's relationship to nature, God, and himself.

When Moses wrote Genesis sometime during Israel's wilderness wanderings, he was not conscious that he was penning the first book of the Bible. He wrote under divine inspiration for all ages to come, to be sure, but his immediate purpose was to write for the benefit of his own generation. He had been commissioned to lead God's people out of Egyptian bondage and to forge them into a priest-nation to be used in God's witness to all nations held in the bonds of paganism and polytheism, the worship of many gods. That Israel needed to be purged of such forms of worship is seen in the incident of the golden calf, a worship of the sacred bull of Egypt (see Exod. 32).

The children of Israel had spent four centuries in a pagan land, the greater part of the time as slaves. The Egyptians worshiped just about everything in the natural order, including the Nile River and its life-giving water, the sun and other heavenly bodies, serpents, birds, bugs (the scarab or sacred beetle), bulls, and men. While at least some of the Israelites retained their knowledge of and worship of the true God, they were contaminated by the pagan religion of their captors. If they were to fulfill their destiny, they must be purified from such and fortified against future contacts with paganism to which subsequent history showed them to be most susceptible.

It is reasonable, therefore, to see that in Genesis 1 Moses was not simply listing certain facts about creation. His purpose went beyond the factual to the theological. The facts were but the vehicle which contained his greater message: that rather than worship the gods of the Egyptians, the Israelites were to worship and serve the true God who created all these things. Moses did not state this in so many words, but one cannot fail to see this as the true message portrayed against the backdrop of the natural order which came from God. The creative record is factual, to be sure, but facts expressed in beautiful poetic language.

The God who inspired Moses to write does not deny the existence of paganism. Rather he recognizes but forbids it, as he says, "Thou shalt have no other gods before me. Thou shalt not make unto thee any graven image" (Exod. 20:3–4). Since these words were spoken three months after the exodus from Egypt, they evidently antedate Moses' writing of Genesis 1. This chapter reflects the monotheism demanded in Exodus 20.

Israel is to worship him who created the heaven and the earth, and not the natural order itself. Israel is not to worship the Nile but the God who created water, not the sun god Ra or other heavenly bodies, but him who spoke them into being; not serpents, bugs, and bulls, but him who created them. Israel is not to regard a pharaoh or any other man as divine; worship belongs only to him who said, "Let us make man." This manifold truth is further emphasized by God's words that man is not to bow down before these things or their material image and likeness, for man is made in the image and likeness of him who created the universe and all that it contains. Rather than to be dominated by *things,* man is given "dominion over the fish of the sea, and over the fowl of the air, and over the cattle, and over all the earth, and over every creeping thing that creepeth upon the earth."

Since Moses wrote within the context of earth-bound man and his capabilities then, there is nothing to forbid man from probing into space as his ability allows. Nature is frugal with its secrets and treasures. There is no more sin in space probing than in digging a well for water, a mine for ore, or boring a hole for oil. The possibility of sin lies not in the probing but in what man does with what he learns.

Seen in its theological light, Genesis 1 is not simply a mystery to be unraveled or facts to be debated. It speaks to modern man as it did to the ancients, for modern men still have their pagan gods. Some bow before primitive idols made of wood and stone;

others in ornate temples before images of false deities. The more sophisticated may worship the gods of sex, wine, and materialism in forms too numerous to list.

Genesis 1 declares that we are not to worship or be dominated by such gods. We are to dominate them as we worship and serve the true God who made them. In dramatic form as the curtain of time is raised, we can hear him who was "in the beginning" saying, "Jehovah our God is one Jehovah: and thou shalt love Jehovah thy God with all thy heart, and with all thy soul, and with all thy might" (Deut. 6:4–5, asv). Listening down the ages, we hear him who was present at creation's dawn saying, "No man can serve two masters: for either he will hate the one, and love the other; or else he will hold to the one, and despise the other. Ye cannot serve God and mammon" (Matt. 6:24).

The Christological Implications

Note has been made of God as the creator, and of the Holy Spirit's work in making a cosmos out of the original chaos. Both, of course, are the work of God who is Spirit. But when we turn to the New Testament, the flower of the Old Testament, the emphasis is upon Christ, the second Person of the Trinity, as the intermediate agent in the creative work.

In the first century A.D. there arose a philosophy called Gnosticism which held that God is absolutely good and matter is absolutely evil. The Gnostics wrestled with the problem as to how the universe came into being since, according to their system of thought, an absolutely good God could not create an absolutely evil universe. To explain creation they posited a series of beings coming out of God in descending order, each having less deity than the one before it. The last being possessed enough deity to create, but so little as to be able to create evil matter. When Gnosticism came into contact with Christianity, it identified this last deity at the bottom of the ladder with Christ.

Obviously this view ran head-on into the Christian view of

Christ. It made him a created being, a demigod, almost a demon. So John in his Gospel and Paul in Colossians (see also 1 John and Eph.) answered this heresy.

John 1:1, 3 reads, literally, "In the beginning always was the Word [Christ], and the Word always was equal with God, and the Word always was God himself. . . . Every single part of the universe through him came into being, and apart from him there came into being not even one thing which has come into being." In two brief verses John declared the coeternity, coequality, and coexistence of Christ with God. As God himself Christ was the intermediate agent creating every single part of the universe from atoms to solar systems. As a mystic, John looked at every single part of the universe and said that as God, Christ created it all in its several parts.

Where did John get his idea for using the term *word* or *logos* for Christ? Some see its meaning as of Greek origin. However, John's Gospel is Hebrew in background. The Dead Sea Scrolls show his thought patterns to be those of Palestine prior to A.D. 70. So we look for a Hebrew meaning for *logos*.

The phrase "in the beginning" of John 1:1 suggests the wording of Genesis 1:1. Therefore we are justified in looking into that context for John's idea. *Logos* or *word* means an open, spoken manifestation of the speaker. Each phase of creative work in Genesis 1 is introduced by the phrase "and God said." There is God's *word* or *Word*. It seems that this is the sense of John's usage who alone used *Word* to refer to Christ, relating him to the creative acts of God. Hence, the *Word* is Christ as the open, spoken manifestation of God, or the intermediate agent in the act of creation.

Paul, on the other hand, thought cosmically. In Colossians 1:15–16, he said of Christ, literally, "Who is the exact representation of the invisible God, Lord of every single part of creation, because in him alone was created the universe as a whole in the heavens and upon the earth, the visible and the invisible . . . the universe as a whole through him and unto him stands created." As God himself, Christ is the *sphere* in which creation took place; he is the *intermediate agent* in creation; and he is the *goal* toward which all creation moves.

Colossians 1:17 adds further to the glory of Christ in the creation. Literally, "And he is before every single part of the universe, and the universe as a whole in him holds together." Before the first atom was created, he always was. And he is the cohesive force which holds the entire universe together.

Through the ages man thought of a geocentric or earth-centered universe. Since the time of Copernicus and Galileo he has thought of a heliocentric or sun-centered universe, but in the light of the modern findings of astronomy this view is no longer tenable. What we once thought of as the *universe*, we now know is only one *solar system* revolving about the sun. One astronomer estimates that there are fourteen quadrillion (14 followed by fifteen zeros) solar systems, each with its own sun.

What or who, then, is the center of the universe? Almost two thousand years ago, writing under divine inspiration, Paul declared that Christ is the center of the universe; it coheres in him. But for the power of Christ the entire universe would explode into nothingness. The cosmos would again become a chaos. The universe is neither geocentric nor heliocentric. It is Christocentric or Christ-centered. The universe centers, not in the *sun*, but in the *Son!* The more we learn about the universe, the more glorious Christ appears.

True science and true theology unite in praising God through his creation. Truly the heavens declare God's glory and demonstrate his handiwork. David wrote more than he knew. For before and beyond the universe by faith we see God—and rest in him.

> Though earth and man were gone,
> And suns and universes ceased to be,
> And Thou wert left alone,
> Every existence would exist in Thee.
> —EMILY BRONTË

2

CREATION'S CROWN

Genesis 1:26–27; 2:7–8, 18, 21–24

BOTH THE BIBLE and science agree that man is the crown of creation. They may differ about the process of how man came to be, but they agree in measure on the product. William Gladstone said, "Man himself is the crowning wonder of creation; the study of his nature the noblest study the world affords."

At the end of the first five stages in creation God saw that it was "good." But having made man, he saw that it was "very good." This suggests that man is someone special in God's creative act and purpose. Henry Giles says, "Man is greater than a world—than systems of worlds; there is more mystery in the union of soul with body than in the creation of a universe."

The phenomenon of man challenges us to probe this mystery. The fact that man is capable of studying himself is one evidence of his greatness in comparison with other elements of the created order. In such a study man asks questions and seeks answers.

Whence Came Man?

A little child asks his mother, "Where did I come from?" He asks more than he realizes, for this is a question which has confronted the greatest minds of the ages. Someone suggested that the important thing is not whence came man but whither he is going. Yet the two questions are inextricably bound together. If man is only an animal, there is no *whither.* Conversely, if man has a *whither* he is more than the product of blind forces. He did not just happen, but is a purposeful creation. And that purpose extends above and beyond the animal nature alone.

The inquiry as to man's origin is of concern to both science and religion. The general trend of science, following the law of continuity, is to regard man as the final result of a long process of evolution—from the minute particles of life in water through various stages into an ape and then to the complex being as man. Some theistic scientists admit the guiding hand of God in the process, while others simply see the law of continuity working impersonally. But in either case an important question must be faced: at what point in the process did man become so far superior to the highest form of creatures before him—and how was it done? Even if one denies man's immortality, he is confronted with man as he is now—a reasoning person with spiritual qualities unknown to any other creature. The very unfulfilled aspirations and dreams of earth-bound man call for life beyond man's earthly existence. In the words of Browning's *Andrea Del Sarto:*

> Ah, but a man's reach should exceed his grasp,
> Or what's a heaven for? . . .

It should be noted, however, that science's tentative answer to the *whence* is nothing more than theory. By the very nature of its manner of inquiry, science can never be in a position to be dogmatic—until a theory without question becomes fact. Science, as such, deals with phenomena. Though its inquiry begins in faith that something unknown can become known, its final conclusions must be based upon fact. To act otherwise involves either faith or fancy. To act on the basis of fancy is unscientific and places the discipline of science in the area of make-believe. To act on faith is not scientific but religious behavior. Once science has established a theory as fact, it becomes truth. And truth, whether found in the laboratory or in the Bible, agrees with itself, for all truth is of God.

The theory of evolution will never become fact until the so-called "missing link" between ape and man is found beyond question of doubt. This search has been one of major scientific emphasis. The once-hailed Piltdown Man has been proved a hoax. The discovery of suggested steps in the evolutionary process, such as Neanderthal Man, has been attempted by building men out of sketchy bits of bone. For instance, a skull of great antiquity is found, one which shows that it belonged to some creature of lesser intelligence than modern man. It is declared to be the skull of a primitive type of man. Perhaps there are other bits of bones with it. The scientist, using his imagination, then proceeds to build a *man* such as he conceives him to have been. No matter how skillfully one reasons, if he starts from the wrong premise, he will arrive at the wrong conclusion. The bones may be those of an ape, not of a man.

I suspect that these efforts to build a man are more acts of fancy than the discovery of fact. In biblical interpretation this is called *eisegesis* rather than *exegesis,* reading preconceived ideas into something rather than drawing out what is in it. The missing link has not been found. On the basis of present fact, one is justified in questioning whether it ever will be. In my limited knowledge and judgment, it will not.

One thing is quite evident: in the creative process, life in an ascending order emerged on different levels. Since then, there is evidence of development within the various species. But there is no evidence that a lower species ever climbed to a higher level. Just as man made in God's image has never become God or even a semigod, so no frog ever became a horse. Science will continue to delve into the mystery. Unfortunately, some will propound theory as though it were fact and, unhappily, multitudes will believe them. But popular acceptance of an opinion does not make it true.

If religion is true to its genius, it must adhere to its scriptures. In the Judeo-Christian faith that means the Bible. Genesis 1:26 reads, "Let us make man in our image, after our likeness: and let them have dominion over the fish of the sea, and over the fowl of the air, and over the cattle, and over all the earth, and over every creeping thing that creepeth upon the earth."

Man is to have dominion over, not evolve from, the creeping things. The Bible clearly declares that man is a direct, special creation of God. Of every other order of life God says, "Let certain things be," but of man he says, "Let us make man" to be over all the rest.

How are we to understand the phrase "let us make"? Of whom or to whom was God speaking? Various suggestions have been made: the heavenly hosts, including angels; the heavenly council; the plural of majesty; the Trinity. Surely the first does not apply, for angels are created beings. The heavenly council is but an adaptation of this idea. The plural of majesty is more plausible. But to me the Trinity is the most satisfactory answer. While there is truth in the objection that such an interpretation reads back into the text the later revelation of God as Father, Son, and Holy Spirit, it is also true that Moses wrote, not out of his reason, but out of God's revelation. May we not then see the later revelation in embryo? The Bible as a whole certainly teaches that the triune God was involved in the creative act.

For a Christian interpretation we are justified in seeing the *us* as a *plurality* in *singularity* of being. The triune God spoke within himself as one, even though the verb form is plural. Elsewhere *Elohim* (e.g., Gen. 1:1), used of God, though it is a plural noun takes the singular verb. Since the Old Testament must be interpreted in the light of the New Testament, it seems justifiable to see here a plurality in singularity. But whatever position one takes, the Bible's answer to the *whence* is that man is a special creation of God. If the special creation idea be objected to on the basis of *make* in 1:26, note should be taken that *created* appears twice in verse 27.

Recently an effort was made in California to require science textbooks dealing with the origin of man to include the biblical as well as the scientific view. An organization of scientists strongly opposed this on the basis that doing so would not be scientific. Not scientific to look at all the evidence in a matter? If something be held as truth, those holding it should not fear letting it stand the test of other ideas. To me this action indicates that the scientists are not as confident of their position as they appear to be. The Bible is not afraid of the searchlight of *truth*.

How are we to understand *man* in the biblical context? In Genesis 1:26, the word *man* (Hebrew, *adham*, note "Adam") is without the definite article, so it could read "mankind." However, in verse 27 it reads "the man," or a particular man (see also 2:7, 15, 16, 18, 19, 20). Beginning in 2:19 "the man" is translated as *Adam* (KJV), although the Revised Standard Version renders it "the man" (but note 3:17 see also J. W. Watts, *A Distinctive Translation of Genesis*, pp. 19–24 for uses of this word).

What may we deduce from this? Some see *man* without the article as referring to symbolic man or mankind. In this sense it could mean that God created other people besides Adam. If so, it would explain Cain's wife (see 4:17). Clyde Francisco (p. 18) suggests the possibility that other people were created *after* Adam and Eve, but he adds that if that be true, their posterity were destroyed in the flood. "All men living today are descendants of Adam through Noah, because only Noah and his family survived the flood."

However, in any case the word *man* in 1:26 simply introduces the idea of mankind. And the fact that he is to have dominion over the rest of God's creation shows that he is not simply derived from it through a process of evolution. He is separate and apart from it, and his destiny is to be above it. Rather than to be dominated by or to worship creation in its various elements, man stands above it as one made in God's image. When he slips from the pedestal upon which God placed him to become subservient to the lower order of things, he has denied his creator and his destiny.

It would be just as correct to translate the phrase "the man" in

Genesis 1:27 by *Adam* as to postpone that translation until Genesis 2:19. The point is that while God created all mankind, he began with *one* man, Adam. Adam is not symbolic man but *representative* man. His moral and spiritual nature and his experience later unfolded in Genesis are that of all men. In Acts 17:26, Paul clearly points to man's beginning as "one." Literally, God "hath made out of one ["blood" not in the best manuscripts] every ethnic group of men." While Moses reserved until Genesis 2:20–25 the account of Eve's origin, he notes that man was made both male and female. They were commanded to "be fruitful, and multiply, and replenish the earth, and subdue it."

Who Is Man?

Man is different from other creatures, for God made him "in our image, after our likeness." Some interpreters make a distinction between *image* and *likeness*. However, Genesis 1:27 uses *image* alone. The statement in verse 26 is a Hebrew parallelism which expresses the same thought in two ways.

But what are we to understand by *image?* Obviously, since God is Spirit, it does not refer to bodily form; it must mean that man is akin to God in spiritual nature. *Image* means an exact duplicate. This does not mean that man is God but that he is like him in nature, possessed of self-conscious reason. Some lower animals have memory but not the ability to reason. Of all God's creatures this ability is given only to man. Francisco (p. 13) notes that while *create* is never used of man in the Bible, man in a sense does create conditions. Animals only adjust to their environment, but man creates his as seen in heated and cooled homes. He does not, through evolution, grow wings, but by reason he deciphers the laws of aerodynamics, so that he builds planes in which he flies like a bird. By the same token he does not develop gills, but he builds submarines to enable him to move beneath the surface of water.

Furthermore, man is a free being. While his instincts play a certain part in his conduct, he is free to choose his course of action but is responsible for his choices. Most of all he is capable of fellowship with God. Therein, above all other things, lies his peculiar dignity and privilege.

However, in Genesis 2 the *who* of man is more clearly set forth. What is found in embryo in Genesis 1:26–27 is seen in its fully developed state in Genesis 2. Some interpreters see chapter 2 as a separate account of creation. Others, including myself, see it as a further development of the account begun in chapter 1. Genesis 2:1–5 gives a resumé of chapter 1 up to the point of the creation of man. Genesis 2:5 closes with the almost plaintive note that there was "not a man to till the ground." Was not this the author's way of saying that without man creation was incomplete?

In Genesis 2:7 Moses writes, "And the Lord God formed man of the dust of the ground, and breathed into his nostrils the breath of life; and man became a living soul." To me the Revised Standard Version falls short in saying that man became "a living being." It seems that God is saying that man bears three relationships.

As one made out of the dust of the ground, man is, in his body, akin to the natural order. The body is composed of various chemical elements, a proper balance of which is conducive to physical health. As a part of the ground, one's body is destined at death to return to it. "For dust thou art, and unto dust shalt thou return" (3:19).

As one into whom God breathed the breath of life, man is related to the animal order. The animal principle of life indwells him, and his body functions like that of other animals. As such, man is destined to die as the animal principle of life flees from him. So, in common with other animals, the human animal will die and his body will return to the elements whence it came—if the Lord delays his return.

But there is something more in man not found in other animals. "Man became a living soul." This part of man is akin to God—made in his image and likeness. Man, therefore, is a person, not a thing. As such he is capable of fellowship with God and is incomplete apart from God. There is finitely in man—in you—an element which responds to that which is in God infinitely. This part of your nature never dies. Spiritually you are destined to live eternally, either in God's fellowship or outside it. As a free moral person, you decide which it shall be. God never coerces; to do that would make you less than a person. The lower animals live by instinct, but man in his highest self lives by reason and choice. This is a tremendous privilege, but an awesome responsibility.

No treatment of the *who* would be complete without considering man's counterpart—woman. "Male and female created he them" (1:27). In 2:18, 21–24 Moses gives the details as to how woman came to be. "And the Lord God said, It is not good that the man should be alone; I will make him an help meet for him." Though man had fellowship with God, there was no one to *correspond to him* at the human level; so God proposed to make *one corresponding to him*. The Hebrew word rendered "help meet" means a helper according to what is in front of him as in a mirror, corresponding to and adequate to himself, that is, a friend, a companion who is conceived as his equal. Woman also is made in God's image and likeness (see 1:26–27).

In beautiful language the writer tells how God placed the man in Eden, a garden of paradise (2:15). Then he brought all beasts and birds to him that he might name them. "But for Adam there was not found an help meet for him." None of these creatures corresponded to him. He was above, not equal to, them—and was left lonely.

Inducing a supernatural sleep upon Adam, God performed the first surgical operation. From Adam's side he took a rib, which he made into a woman. As one has said, he took the rib from underneath Adam's arm that he might protect her, and from his bosom that he might love her. He did not take a bone from Adam's head, that she might rule over him, or from his foot, that he might rule over her. But God took the bone from Adam's bosom, his side, that she might be his equal, corresponding to him, to stand by his side in joy and sorrow, victory and defeat. She is to be the object of his affection, the wife of his bosom, and the darling of his heart.

When God brought the woman to Adam, he exclaimed, "This is it, this time." The Revised Standard Version reads, "This at last is bone of my bones and flesh of my flesh; she shall be called Woman, because she was taken out of Man" (2:23). Unlike the animals that God had brought to him, woman corresponded to man in nature. She was the one for whom he had been looking and longing. She was/is his complement, taken from him, but different from him—his likeness in nature as made in God's image, but different in sex and function. One is incomplete without the other.

In the first marriage ceremony God said, "Therefore shall a man leave his father and his mother, and shall cleave unto his wife: and they shall be one flesh" (2:24). Jesus cited this as God's original intent in marriage (Matt. 19:5). One man and one woman, until death does them part. Any deviation from this is contrary to God's intentional will.

It is in the human constitution as well as in God's will that man and woman need each other, and the divine ideal is one man and one woman as husband and wife. When a man and a woman marry, they bring into being something which never existed before—their own home. They should stand together against anyone or anything which threatens its well-being. I have often counseled young people contemplating marriage that should the time come when they might be forced to choose between each other and their parents, they have already made that choice at the marriage altar.

Alone, a man and a woman are incomplete, physically, morally, and spiritually. But together in every sense they are fulfilled and strong. If woman needs man's protection, it is just as true that he needs hers. John Ruskin has stated this beautifully and effectively: "The buckling on of a knight's armor by his lady's hand was not a mere caprice of romantic fashion. It is the type of an eternal truth that the soul's armor is never well set to the heart unless a woman's hand has braced it, and it is only when she braces it loosely that the honor of manhood fails."

Adam and Eve together in marital bliss in a paradise prepared by God for them—this was the divine intent. It might well still be today, if the story had ended with, "They lived happily ever after." Such was God's will. But through the rebellion of man's free will, tragedy loomed ahead.

Why?

In view of this foreboding, *why* did God create man? For one thing, God never does anything halfway. Since man is the crown of creation, he was necessary to complete God's creative work. But the full answer to the *why* runs far deeper than this. Knowing that they invite anxiety, heartache, and maybe tragedy, why do a husband and wife bring children into the world? Is it not because in a man and a woman is a kind of love which calls for expression, and which is not satisfied even in their love for each other?

It is hardly sufficient to say in the words of James Weldon Johnson's *God's Trombones* that God was lonely, so he made man. For God had his creation, angels, and the *plurality* in *singularity* in his person. But God is love, and love to be expressed calls for an object. God is more than self-love; his is also an other-love. That other-love could find its fitting object only in one who corresponds finitely to that which God is infinitely. Therefore, God created man in his image and likeness, because neither angels nor a natural creation could respond appropriately to God's love in the sense of his love for man.

This is not to say that God is not complete within himself, but God's acts must be interpreted in the light of his overall revelation in the Scriptures. The Bible clearly teaches that God's greatest glory is expressed in his redeeming love, so we are justified in seeing his next-highest glory in his creating love, especially his creation of man.

Simply stated, God created man for the purpose of *fellowship*. This is seen in his daily walk in the garden of Eden (see 3:8). It is seen in the brief biography of Enoch (see 5:24). It is seen in the broken heart of God when that fellowship was marred through man's sin. The Bible is filled with the laments of this infinite Lover after his faithless beloved.

This purpose of fellowship is also seen in the emptiness of man apart from it. This very emptiness drives man to distraction as he rushes hither and yon in search of satisfaction. As God was not fully satisfied with the worlds he had made, so man is never satisfied by the material when his grandest nature is spiritual. Augustine touched the heart of the matter in his autobiographical statement that since man is made for God, his soul is ever restless until it finds rest in him.

Why did God create man? The answer is seen in his seeking love. He is ever walking through this world calling "Where art thou?" to wayward men. It is at this point that the Judeo-Christian religion differs from all others. In the latter, man is seeking God; in the former, God is seeking man. Jesus stated his own mission as "to seek and to save that which was lost" (Luke 19:10). To be lost is to be separated from someone. Jesus came to look for, find, and bring back to the Father man who was lost from him—back to a restored fellowship.

This is the sense of reconciliation. Never does the Bible speak of God needing to be reconciled to man, it is always man being reconciled to God (see 2 Cor. 5:20). A mother says to her child, "If you are not good, God will not love you." This simply is not true. God loves us whether or not we are good. "God commendeth his love toward us, in that, while we were yet sinners, Christ died for us" (Rom. 5:8). In so doing he created the conditions whereby, in keeping with his holy, righteous nature, he might offer forgiveness to all who in faith will receive it. And all who do he clasps to his bosom in a restored fellowship—the condition in which and for which he created man in the beginning.

Whither?

The final question is *whither?* When God created man, he gave him dominion over his creation. Through the centuries man has done a pretty good job of subduing the natural creation (see Ps. 8:5–8). Citing this promise from Psalm 8, the author of Hebrews notes, "But now we see not yet all things put under him" (Heb. 2:8). He is thinking here not of the natural but of the spiritual universe. In that area man has failed miserably.

And then the author adds, "But we see Jesus" (Heb. 2:9). In his death and resurrection Jesus has opened the door that man may fully realize his destiny of spiritual triumph over all that opposes God and man. And in such triumph he may once again know the warm fellowship with God for which he was created. Revelation 22 pictures heaven in terms of a restored Eden. To that blessed state man is invited to move. The God who created us in his image wills to restore that image in Christ. In heaven the glorious bliss depicted in Eden will be eternal, an unmarred fellowship between God and redeemed man.

Thomas Carlyle put it in beautiful, simple words. "The older I grow, and I now stand on the brink of eternity—the more comes back to me that sentence in the catechisms I learned as a child, and the fuller and deeper its meaning becomes: 'What is the chief end of man? To glorify God and enjoy him forever.'"

3

CREATION'S CURSE

Genesis 3:1–24

ADAM AND EVE alone inhabited the garden of Eden, for the beasts were left outside. But, alas, they were not alone for long! Soon the serpent entered the garden—"gatecrasher," someone has called it. However it came to be in the garden, the serpent's presence set in motion events which have cursed God's "very good" creation ever since. Through the ages men have sought to discover the origin of evil. The Bible makes no such attempt, at least not formally. It accepts the fact of evil, and shows how it has operated in history, blighting everything it has touched. It is truly creation's curse.

The Tempter

Though the name *Satan* does not appear in the story, it is evident from the overall teachings of the Bible that he is present and acting through the serpent. It is not my purpose to probe the mystery as to the origin of Satan. Since God alone is eternal, it may be assumed that Satan is a created being. Since God's creation was "good," it follows that Satan was not originally evil. Some interpreters see Isaiah 14:12–14 and Ezekiel 28:11–19 as references to how he became the evil one. Though these passages were directed to pagan rulers, there are elements which could apply to Satan. Evidently he is a fallen angel who, out of ambition and pride, sought to overthrow his Creator. He and those who followed him were cast out of heaven. In the spiritual realm of the universe as well as in the arena of earth, Satan still seeks to overthrow God. On earth he seeks to dethrone God by perverting man's loyalty. As one may hurt the parent most by harming the child, so Satan seeks to strike at God where it will hurt him most—by striking at man.

Regardless of how we explain the evil one, his earthly presence is evident. Among other things, the Bible calls him Satan (adversary), Devil (slanderer), and Apollyon (destroyer). As Satan, he is the adversary of both God and man. As Devil, he slanders God to man (Gen. 3) and man to God (Job 1–2). As Apollyon, he seeks to destroy God, man, and every good. Jesus called him a "murderer" or man-killer, a liar and the father of every lie (John 8:44). He also called him "the prince of this world" (John 12:31). Paul refers to him as "the god of this world" or age (2 Cor. 4:4). He also speaks of him as "the prince of the power of the air, the spirit that now worketh in the children of disobedience" (Eph. 2:2). Revelation 12:9 sums it all up in speaking of him as "the great dragon . . . that old serpent, called the Devil, and Satan, which deceiveth the whole world: he was cast out into the earth, and his angels were cast out with him." From the Greek text, "old serpent" may also be translated "original serpent."

Atkinson (p. 41) draws the following conclusion about Satan. "It seems impossible to assemble all that the Bible says about him without coming to the conclusion that he is a super-human personal being of a high order, created perfect like all God's creatures, but the author of evil through the conception of an evil thought and the formation of an evil choice in his will."

Evil entered God's created order not through inanimate objects or the seducing of beasts, but through the seduction of man who was made in God's image and endowed with the right of choice between good and evil.

In dramatic fashion Moses sets the stage for the earthly struggle between Satan and man. He strikes the note of expectancy by saying that the serpent was "more subtil than any beast of the field" (Gen. 3:1). Subsequent events show it to be more subtle than man himself. Was this not due to the fact that Satan had chosen to think through the serpent? Man's only hope in coping with Satan is through the mind of Christ.

More to the point is the fact that Satan himself appeared in the form of a serpent. That this creature was not a snake crawling on the ground is evident from the curse later placed upon it (3:14). So evidently it was an upright being, possibly birdlike. At any rate it was a graceful, beautifully colored, appealing creature. Satan has many disguises. In the Bible he never appears to man as Satan, but to God he always appears as Satan. He can deceive man, but God knows him for who he is.

Paul says that Satan even transforms himself into an angel of light (2 Cor. 11:14). He always appears to man with grand and glorious promises, but they are promises which he neither can nor intends to fulfill. For instance, he does not point out an alcoholic to a young man and say, "I will make you like him." Instead he points to a "man of distinction." To a young lady he does not point to a prostitute and say, "I will make you like she is." Rather he points to a beautiful social butterfly who is popular with the opposite sex. But once either takes his bait, if he has his way, he will produce an alcoholic and/or a prostitute. One should beware of Satan's siren song, for it is the dirge of death to those who are ensnared by it.

One of the enigmas of life is our difference in attitude toward material and moral and spiritual matters. In material matters, each generation learns from previous ones and then builds upon their foundation. But when it comes to moral and spiritual concerns, we ignore the lessons of history, as each generation insists upon making its own mistakes. Thus the cycle of evil goes on and on. Each *Adam* and *Eve* insists upon learning the hard way that the wages of sin is death. Nevertheless, it is the duty of God's spokesmen to warn men.

The Temptation

When God placed Adam in the garden of Eden, he permitted him to eat the fruit of every tree in the garden, save one —"the tree of the knowledge of good and evil" (Gen. 2:17). The day that he ate of this tree, man would surely die. This warning was given to Adam before Eve was formed, which explains why Satan made his initial approach to Eve. Adam had this warning firsthand. Eve had it secondhand, evidently from Adam.

Before examining the temptation itself, we must first ask why God permitted it to take place. We may be certain that the serpent did not enter Eden without God's knowledge. Did it do so with his permission? And for a purpose?

It is impossible, in the light of present knowledge, to escape the parallel between the temptation experiences of the first Adam and Jesus Christ, the second Adam (see Matt. 4; 1 Cor. 15:45). Furthermore, in considering the workings of Satan, one cannot ignore the dramatic scenes in the prelude to Job. There God permitted Satan to test Job as to the basis of the patriarch's righteousness. Satan slandered him to God by saying that he served God only for what he could get out of him; so God *permitted* Satan to put Job to the test. As always, he allowed Satan to go so far but no farther (Job 1:8–12; 2:3–6). Had the adversary brought accusations against Adam and Eve as he did against Job? If so, it is understandable that God would permit them to be *tempted* or *tested* (the Hebrew word may be translated either way). God *tests* men to prove them genuine; Satan *tempts* men to prove them false. If Satan had slandered man to God, we may assume that God permitted him to put man to the test in order that he might have the opportunity to prove Satan's slander false.

Philosophically, there is another possibility. Matthew 4:1 says that the Holy Spirit led Jesus into the wilderness "to be tempted of the devil." "To be tempted" is an infinitive of purpose, which shows that God, not Satan, took the initiative in this temptation experience. Jesus was God's Son and the Messiah; yet he was also man. In his humanity he was tested as to the kind of Messiah he would be. Would he follow God's will or Satan's will? The record shows that he was faithful in every sense to God's will.

Now God had created man in a state of innocence. He was neither moral nor immoral, but amoral. To be righteous man must have the opportunity to choose whether to be righteous or unrighteous. Such a choice is involved in God's prohibition to eat of the forbidden tree. It is reasonable to see God permitting Satan to offer man the choice between obeying God's will or Satan's will. Alas, while the Devil failed with Jesus, he succeeded with Adam and Eve, and they became unrighteous.

To Eve, Satan said, "Yea, hath God said, Ye shall not eat of every tree of the garden?" (Gen. 3:1). "Yea, hath God said?" may better read, "Did God actually say?" Also *every* more properly reads *any*. In one brief question Satan questioned both God's word and his goodness. This explains why he tempted Eve when she was alone. Adam had heard the prohibition directly from God; Eve had heard it from Adam. It was a simple thing, therefore, to place doubt in her mind as to the exactness of God's word.

This is the first question recorded in the Bible, and it was asked by Satan. Donald Grey Barnhouse (vol. 1, p. 18) notes that "there would never have been any need for a question, if sin had not come." He notes also that this is the first denial of divine revelation and divine inspiration. Did God actually say this? Or was it simply Adam's or man's idea? Eve was not present when it was said, so how could she be certain that this was really God's word?

Satan has been whispering these words of doubt into men's ears and hearts ever since. Once such doubts find root in one's life, he or she is not certain about any word from the Lord. Everything becomes relative. There is no basic standard of conduct such as the Ten Commandments, and the gospel itself becomes a question mark rather than an exclamation point. A world lost in confusion longs to hear a "thus saith the Lord" rather than the speculations of men.

Someone described a liberal preacher as one who from a looseleaf Bible preaches on "The Ten Suggestions." Satan would turn every Bible into a looseleaf edition whose pages can be discarded at will. He would leave every man to drift on a stormy sea of uncertainty, driven and tossed by every contrary wind of doctrine.

Not only did the evil one plant the seed of doubt as to God's word, but also as to his goodness. God in his benevolence had provided for all of man's need. His prohibition involved only one tree, but Satan broadened it to include every tree. To say the least, he pointed to the one forbidden tree while ignoring all the others. In other words, he said, "God is holding out on you. He is a miser. Even if he said this, he is neither good nor fair. If all this were mine, I would share it. But God—well, he does not love you."

Satan is still saying the same thing to men and women. A young woman echoed the Devil's words when she said that the Ten Commandments are but words written by ancient men in order to make people be good. Even so, the "Thou shalt nots" are shown to be those of a negative psychology, rather than guardian angels to warn men of tragedy in ignoring them.

Satan continues to whisper into gullible hearts, "God is holding out on you." God has endowed us with basic instincts for our good. Some say that the Devil tempts us in our lower nature. To the contrary, he tempts us in our higher nature. He endeavors to get us to express our God-given instincts in a way not intended by God. Years ago my seminary professor, W. Hersey Davis, said that sin is an illegitimate expression of a legitimate desire.

A young man who was my college contemporary sought to justify his illicit sex life by saying that God gave him his sex desire and intended for him to satisfy it. In the same manner Satan leads men to pervert every benevolent instinct. Thrift becomes miserliness, the acquisitive instinct becomes covetousness and thievery, and the protective instinct becomes aggression and war.

A current psychology teaches that to say no to a child warps his personality. This is another of Satan's lies. Much of the rebellion among youth may be traced to the practice of this psychology in the rearing of children. This kind of training leads to the attitude which says if one has a desire, express it. Divine inhibitions go out the window. We would do well to heed James 1:14–15, which reads literally, "But everyone is tempted by his own [natural God-given] desire, being lured out of a place of safety and baited like a fish. Then when lust [God-given desire perverted] hath conceived it births sin, and sin reaching its full development, brings forth the abortion of death." It is no wonder that James added, "Stop being led astray, my beloved brethren" (James 1:16). If only Eve and Adam had heeded this warning!

But give Eve credit for one thing—she did strive to correct Satan's lie (Gen. 3:2–3). She avowed God's goodness in permitting them to eat of all trees in the garden, save one. Of that one tree God had said, "Ye shall not eat of it, neither shall ye touch it, lest ye die." Note that "neither shall ye touch it" is not in God's words to Adam (2:16–17). Some accuse Eve of adding to God's word, but perhaps she and Adam had agreed that they should not even touch the tree because of the dire circumstances involved. The best way to avoid sin is to avoid temptation. One should never toy with evil but flee from it as though it were the Devil himself. Someone said, "To pray against temptation, and yet rush into occasion, is to thrust your fingers into the fire, and then pray they might not be burnt."

In reply Satan said, "Ye shall not surely die" (3:4). He moved from questioning God's word and goodness to calling God a liar. Imagine the father of lies calling the God of truth a liar! Yet Satan still seeks to turn the truth of God into a lie. He denies the inspiration and truth of the Bible, the love of God, the deity and virgin birth of Jesus, his blood atonement and bodily resurrection, the immortality of the soul, the final judgment, and the reality of hell. But the wreckage of men and nations along every mile of history eloquently declares that God is true and Satan is a liar. Strange to say, however, men are still gullible to Satan's lies and indifferent to God's truth.

At this point the evil one delivered his "Sunday punch." "For God doth know that in the day ye eat thereof, then your eyes shall be opened, and ye shall be as gods, knowing good and evil" (3:5). This is the climax of Satan's slander of God's word and goodness. He was trying to deprive man of his full potential.

The word *gods* renders *Elohim*, the name for God in Genesis 1:1. It may refer to "gods," but in this context "God" is the better translation. Speaking of man, Psalm 8:5 says, "For thou hast made him a little lower than God." (The King James Version translates *Elohim* as "angels" in this verse, but the Revised Standard Version has "God.") Made in God's image, man is a little lower than God. Sin results when he tries to be God. The basis of all sin is self-centeredness. Someone has noted that the middle letter of *sin* is *i*—sIn—and the greater the *I*, the greater the sin. Man sins when he centers his life in himself rather than in God. To make one's will predominant over God's will is rebellion against God. Such an effort to be God was involved in Satan's fall, and he ever seeks to get men to follow his own abortive effort.

Through sin, Adam and Eve did not become God but were separated from him. However, they did learn "good and evil." They knew the absence of good and the destructive power of evil. What the Devil said was true, only in a far different sense than he intended. God knows good to love it; he knows evil to abhor it. Man knows evil only to practice it, and good only to lose it.

Satan had done his work well, and Eve was ready for the kill. "And when the woman saw that the tree was good for food, and that it was pleasant to the eyes, and a tree to be desired to make one wise, she took of the fruit thereof, and did eat, and gave also unto her husband with her; and he did eat" (Gen. 3:6). She should not touch it, but she did. More, she took it. Forbidden to eat it, she ate it, and she led her husband to do likewise. One never sins in isolation, for sin has social aspects. One person's sinful act affects others.

In this one verse we find the entire scope of temptation or the areas in which Satan tempts us. One is *physical appetite*—"the tree was good for food." Another is the *aesthetic* nature—"it was pleasant to the eyes." The third is *ambition*—"a tree desired to make one wise." In these areas the Devil tempted Jesus (Matt. 4): "Command that these stones be made bread" (physical appetite, Matt. 4:3); "Cast thyself down," do the exciting, the risque, (aesthetic nature, Matt. 4:6); "all these things will I give thee" (ambition, Matt. 4:9). Luke 4:13 speaks of "all" or every kind of temptation. Hebrews 4:15 says that Jesus "was in all points tempted like as we are, yet without sin." John expresses these three areas as "the lust of the flesh, and the lust of the eyes, and the pride of life" (1 John 2:16). Every kind of temptation may be fitted into one of these three categories. They are the same areas in which Satan tempts us today—he has no new ones. Indeed, why should he, since, with the exception of Jesus, he catches all others with the same old bait? Still he deludes us into thinking that sin is up-to-date, the *in thing*, when all the while it is as old-fashioned as Eden.

When Jesus told his disciples to fish for men, he always spoke in terms of net-fishing. The language of James 1:14 ("is drawn away," lured out of a place of safety; "enticed" RSV, baited as a fish) is that of hook-and-line fishing. It is thus that Satan fishes for men, and he knows just the right bait to catch each person. If you rise above physical appetite, he catches you in your aesthetic nature or ambition, even spiritual ambition. It is no wonder that 1 Peter 5:8 warns us to "be sober, be vigilant; because your adversary the devil, as a roaring lion, walketh about, seeking whom he may devour." However, Satan never appears as a roaring lion, but as an angel of light—that is, until he has caught his prey.

Satan succeeded with Adam and Eve, and he succeeds with us. He failed with Jesus, which suggests that Jesus is our only hope before this adversary. If James tells us how the Devil fishes for men, he also tells us how to avoid being caught. "Submit yourselves therefore to God. Resist the devil, and he will flee from you" (James 4:7). How often Satan leads us to quote the latter half of this verse, while omitting the former half. If we resist the Devil in our strength alone, he will win every time. God says that we are to submit to him, then resist the Devil and he will flee from us. Because Eve and Adam did not *submit*, they were unable to *resist*. As their children, we follow in their fatal path.

What was the nature of this first sin? Some see it as the sexual act, but this hardly holds for two reasons. When Eve sinned, she was not with Adam. Furthermore, the biblical view of sex is such that this would not have been a sin between husband and wife (Gen. 1:28; 2:24). Atkinson (p. 45) attributes this view to the medieval idea, related to heathen asceticism, which elevated celibacy and virginity and equated them with chastity, regarding all sexual desire as evil. This does not coincide with the scriptural view and intent of sex. Others regard the entire story as a myth, a vehicle by which to teach a spiritual truth.

I see the story as a real historical event. There were two actual trees, the tree of knowledge and the tree of life, in a real garden of Eden. Whatever kind of fruit the tree of knowledge bore (not an apple), it was forbidden fruit. The sin of our first parents was rebellion against the expressed will of God, as indeed, is all sin. They faced the choice between God's will and Satan's will. And they chose to do the latter. If this seems to be a *small* sin, there is no such in God's sight. Sin is crossing God's will. What one does after the crossing is secondary.

Shakespeare reminds us in *Measure for Measure* (Act 2, sc. 1) that

> 'Tis one thing to be tempted . . . ,
> Another thing to fall.

Jesus spoke of sin as taking place in the will before it does in the body (Matt. 5:27–28). You may give the consent of your will and not commit the overt act due to lack of opportunity or fear of the consequences. But once you give the consent of your will, that is sin. Today, as in Eden, the battle is fought within the will of man. We are free to choose between God's way and Satan's way, but we are responsible for our choice.

The Tragedy of Sin

It is hardly necessary to speculate as to why Adam joined Eve in her sin. The fact is that he did. And in this first sin Adam and Eve loosed upon the world an avalanche of evil and suffering which defies description. You have but to read the daily paper to see how this destruction continues to roll down the corridors of history. In the events immediately following the first sin or the fall of man we find in embryo the future experience of every man and woman. As Iago puts it in Shakespeare's *Othello* (Act 2, sc. 3):

> When devils will their blackest sins put on,
> They do suggest at first with heavenly shows.

Satan presented to Eve what seemed to be a heavenly show, but it had a hellish ending.

For one thing, sin resulted in *self-consciousness* rather than God-consciousness. "And the eyes of them both were opened, and they knew that they were naked; and they sewed fig leaves together, and made themselves aprons" (Gen. 3:7). The devil opened their eyes, but not to becoming as God, but rather to shame. No longer innocent, they were unrighteous. Their physical nakedness suggests their greater nakedness of soul. Theirs was the self-consciousness of guilty hearts. Naked before God, they were the objects of his wrathful judgment. They made aprons more to hide their nakedness from God than from each other. But robes of self-righteousness are never sufficient to hide guilt from God, for they are as filthy rags in God's sight (Isa. 64:6). Later God hid the nakedness of Adam and Eve by making coats of skin, which involved the death of an innocent victim (Gen. 3:21). This eloquently suggests that man's sin can be hidden from God only by the death of the innocent One whose vicarious atonement alone can cover the sins of man.

Furthermore, sin resulted in a *broken fellowship* with God. "And they heard the voice [sound] of the Lord God walking in the garden in the cool of the day: and Adam and his wife hid themselves from the presence of the Lord God amongst the trees of the garden" (3:8).

The rustling sound of God walking in the garden had been a welcomed one—but no longer. The sinful pair anticipated not fellowship but judgment. In fear rather than in awe they sought to hide themselves among the trees. They used the things given for their good to barricade themselves from God.

It was not only foolish but futile for Adam and Eve to think they could hide from God. Yet we still endeavor to do so—in our intellectual denials of God's existence and the truth of the Bible, in worldly pleasure, and in prosperity which tends to numb the spiritual senses. God, however, looks through the masquerade to see our sinful hearts, and he ever calls to us, "Where art thou?" (3:9).

"Where art thou?" This was God's first question to man. His call to Adam was not to learn his hiding place, for he knew. Rather it was to cause Adam to face his sin. The most difficult words for anyone to utter are "I have sinned." To avoid even the word *sin* modern man has coined substitutes: error, mistake, ignorance, glandular disturbance, social maladjustment, economic need, and even the philosophical upward stumbling in the progress of the race. But the word *sin* belies all of these. Adam and Eve were physically perfect, had full knowledge of God's will, were perfectly mated, and dwelt in a paradise with every need satisfied. Instead of an upward stumbling in progress, they fell down from their exalted state to fail miserably in their potential. None of man's modern evasions satisfies the situation then or now. Sin is rebellion in the heart against God's will and way. Recall that Jesus successfully resisted Satan while hungry and in a wilderness.

Unlike David in his great sin, Adam did not fall down before God and plead for mercy and forgiveness (Ps. 51). Instead, he said that because of his nakedness he was afraid of God, and hid himself (Gen. 3:10). To which God replied, "Who told thee that thou wast naked?" (3:11). God knew that Adam's guilty conscience had told him, and therefore he pinned him down to the exactness of his sin. In the form of a question, God accused Adam of eating the forbidden fruit. He knew this all the while, but a loving God wanted Adam to confess his sin. Only in this manner could he be forgiven.

Adam was caught with no way of escape. He admitted that he had eaten the fruit (3:12), but notice that he preceded his admission with an alibi: "The woman whom thou gavest to be with me, she gave me of the tree, and I did eat." Rather than face his guilt, Adam tried to pass the buck to his wife. Here the man failed to act manly. Rather than protect his wife, he tried to make her the scapegoat. But ultimately he blamed God. In effect he said, "If you had not given me this woman, I would not be in this fix." Everyone, even God, was to blame—but not Adam. Or so he said. Failing to hide behind a tree, he sought to hide behind his wife. He tried to blame his sin on God's *mistake*. He was like the man who blames God for illicit sex because of the appetite "thou gavest to be with me."

The Lord God then faced Eve with her sin. Like Adam, but

with more justification, she passed the buck to the serpent which beguiled her. But also she said, "I did eat." Both Adam and Eve admitted their sin but refused to accept responsibility for it. That is hardly confession, the basis upon which to receive forgiveness (1 John 1:9).

God did not ask the serpent why it had done this. He knew Satan for who he is: a liar and the father of lies, adversary, slanderer, and destroyer. Instead, God began to pronounce judgment. The once beautiful serpent would henceforth crawl on the ground and eat its dust. Actually, a snake does not eat dust, but this depicts Satan's utter defeat. Though through the centuries his evil efforts may seem to succeed before men, God works in all things for good to those who love him and are committed to his will.

The curse upon the woman was twofold. She would bear children in "sorrow" or pain (Gen. 3:16). Someone asked if children would have been born to Adam and Eve if they had not sinned. The answer is yes (1:28; 2:24), but it would have been without pain. The curse lies not in childbearing but in the pain henceforth connected with it. Every time a woman agonizes in childbirth, it should serve as a reminder of sin. Furthermore, the wife would be subject to her husband. Her failure to cope with life's crises apart from her husband placed her in subjection under him. This does not mean that man is to oppress her but to protect her, as Paul clearly shows in Ephesians 5:22–30.

Through the centuries man has abused his position in this regard, at times making woman mere chattel. But Christ has set the standard for his people. The wife is still subject to her husband—but in the Lord—and that makes all the difference in the world. From being man's footstool Jesus has elevated woman to her rightful position as queen of the home. In such position she is still the one corresponding to man, his complement and companion. If anyone should love and serve Christ, surely it is woman.

The curse placed upon man was not work (Gen. 3:17–19), for Adam had work to do in Eden (2:15). Only there he did not tire in his work. In the same manner saints will serve the Lord in heaven (Rev. 22:3), else heaven would become hell. Idleness and boredom are far worse than honest toil.

The curse upon Adam was that a once friendly nature would be hostile to him. "Cursed is the ground because of you" (Gen. 3:17, RSV). In a way beyond our comprehension the natural universe fell when man fell. It came under the limited control of Satan, the prince of the world. Though the universe still moves according to God's laws, Satan uses his power to seek to pervert its goodness. This explains nature on the prowl, such as storms, earthquakes, and the like (see Job 1:19). What the law calls "acts of God" are really acts of Satan.

Thorns and thistles shall grow where man must till the soil. The tares were sown among the wheat by the archenemy Satan (Matt. 13:25, 28, 39). Weeds grow abundantly on their own, but man must fight them as by the sweat of his brow he cultivates his crops.

Alas, man did know good and evil—the absence of the good and the power of evil—and he soon learned evil's penalty. The man and his wife were driven from Eden, "lest he . . . take also of the tree of life, and eat, and live for ever" (Gen. 3:22). Actually, this was an act of God's mercy even though it was mingled with his wrath. When man sinned, he became subject to age, corruption, disease, and pain. Just suppose that in such a condition man could not die. It would be a living hell itself to exist eternally in a body which grew ever feebler, more corrupt, diseased, and painful.

Man, made for God's fellowship, was driven from it. Thus his spirit was dead in trespasses and sins (see Eph. 2:1). Physically, Adam lived many years thereafter; so the death of which God spoke was primarily spiritual, separation from God's fellowship.

It should be noted, however, that God tempers judgment with

mercy. Before he pronounced sentence upon Adam and Eve, he promised a Savior from sin. Forgiveness was in God's heart before sin entered man's heart.

To the serpent he said, "And I will put enmity between thee and the woman, and between thy seed and her seed; it shall bruise thy head, and thou shalt bruise his heel" (Gen. 3:15). This verse has been called the *Protevangelium,* the first gospel. It is the full gospel in embryo. The seed of the woman may best be understood as the virgin-born Jesus Christ. The struggle thus depicted is that between Christ and Satan, both cosmic and earthly. To bruise or crush the head suggests total destruction. To bruise the heel means damage but not destruction. While Satan will damage Christ, with the climax of his evil work being experienced at Calvary, ultimately Christ will win complete victory. Judging by events of the moment, one may wonder, but seen in the light of salvation history, Christ's victory is certain. And his victory will be shared by all who trust in him.

The Bible does not say it specifically, but the spiritual tenor is that Adam and Eve believed this promise and were saved, looking forward in faith to him who would be the seed of the woman.

The early beginning which sounds the uncertain note of tragedy also carries the overtone of hope. God will not fail in his purpose. And though man's sin would one day nail the beloved Son to a cross, beyond it lay the resurrection, ascension, and occupied throne. All who believe in Christ as Savior will be saved, restored to God's fellowship. As in a way not understood by us, the universe fell when man fell, so the Bible teaches that Christ also will redeem the natural order (see Rom. 8:19–25). Having redeemed both the natural and spiritual universe (those who believe in him), Christ will present it to the Father that God may be all in all (1 Cor. 15:25–28).

Innocent man began in a garden of paradise. Redeemed man finally comes to another garden of paradise (Rev. 22:1–5). No cherubim will keep him from the tree of life (Gen. 3:24). For in the new paradise the tree of life will be "on either side of the river" (Rev. 22:2), accessible to all who dwell therein. There, redeemed men will be not God, but sons of God, knowing only good, for evil will not be present. "And the devil that deceived them was cast into the lake of fire and brimstone . . . and shall be tormented day and night for ever and ever" (Rev. 20:10). "And whosoever was not found written in the book of life was cast into the lake of fire" (Rev. 20:15).

As a roaring lion, Satan still stalks the earth, bringing his curse upon everything and everyone who succumbs to his power. God's saints suffer Satan's ravages, but are saved and safe in Christ. We look forward in faith to joining that innumerable throng which forever praises God for his creation (Rev. 4:11), and Christ for his redemption (Rev. 5:9–10).

"Worthy is the Lamb that was slain to receive power, and riches, and wisdom, and strength, and honour, and glory, and blessing. . . . Blessing, and honour, and glory, and power, be unto him that sitteth upon the throne [God the Father], and unto the Lamb [God the Son] for ever and ever" (Rev. 5:12–13).

4

SIN WILL OUT

Genesis 4:1–16

IF GENESIS 1–3 are chapters of *beginning*, Genesis 4 is the chapter of *rebeginnings*. Adam and Eve had been driven from Eden. The image of God in them had been marred by sin. In such condition they could not have unbroken fellowship with God. In a sense, though God was still mindful of man, man was left to himself in a hostile creation. Having defied God's will, he was captive to Satan's will, and the sin which seemed to be so small in its deed, soon raised its ugly head. Sin never lessens but grows worse in degree.

Chapter 4 is a chapter of *firsts*: the first sexual intercourse, conception, and birth; the first agricultural and pastoral work; the first offering to God; the first murder; the first city; the first polygamy; the first musician, the first industry; the first public worship; and man's first question, "Am I my brother's keeper?"

Faithless

Following their expulsion from Eden, Adam and Eve produced their first child. Contrary to later custom found in the Bible, he was named by his mother. She called him Cain, saying, "I have gotten a man from the Lord" (Gen. 4:1). The meaning of the word *Cain* is disputed. It comes from the Hebrew verb *qanah*. Some see the name to mean "one gotten" or "acquired." Davies (p. 144) rejects this reading, stating that *Cain* means spear or

54

reed. He notes that "with the help of" is an English addition, but notes that the sense of it is probably correct. Eve felt that the first child was hers by the help of Jehovah. It is interesting to note that whereas Genesis 1 uses *Elohim* or God and Genesis 2–3 uses the combination *Yahweh Elohim*, Jehovah God, Genesis 4 uses *Yahweh* or Jehovah alone. *Jehovah* distinguishes the true God from pagan gods, it is his saving or redeeming name. *Jesus* means "Jehovah saves."

In due time Eve bore another son, Abel. *Abel* means "breath," "vapor," or "vanity." It is possible that it reflects his parents' realization concerning the vanity of human existence. According to Charles F. Pfeiffer (p. 24), "They had come to realize the results of sin in the created world." However, looking back from later events, the name prophetically denotes the brevity of Abel's life on earth. Cain and Abel were not twins, like Esau and Jacob, as some suggest. They had different natures and temperaments. Abel was a shepherd and Cain a farmer—the most primitive occupations of man. Did the two brothers select their type of work, or was Abel given the easier task since he was the younger? The suggestion is that they chose according to their natures. Subsequent developments indicate religious overtones in their differing occupations.

At any rate, "in process of time" or, literally, "at the end of days," they brought offerings to Jehovah. Though unrecorded, probably Jehovah had set a time and place for this to be done, in a sense, a day and place for formal worship. This may or may not have been a sabbath day. The law of the sabbath came ages later (Exod. 20:8–11), so we are not necessarily bound to that day here. In this context the time is not as important as the occasion.

Each brother brought that which he had: Cain, the fruit of the ground; Abel, the firstlings of his flock and the fat thereof. The fat was regarded as favored by the Lord (Lev. 1:8; 3:3–4; Num. 18:17). Barnhouse (vol. 1, p. 31) suggests the following interpretation: "Abel brought the firstlings and the fattest ones too! He did not pick a scrawny, ill-favored beast, but brought first-born lambs, and the finest. Nothing is too good for God. . . . To give up the undesirable, the unwanted, or the superfluous is not surrender. There must be true sacrifice."

A woman said, "It looks like that old hen is going to die. I believe that I will give her to the preacher." This was not sacrifice or worship, not even love for God's servant. It was more a culling of the flock. But Abel brought the best that he had. Does this mean that Cain chose his gift at random?

For whatever reason, God accepted Abel's offering but rejected Cain's. How these acts of the Lord were manifested is not stated. Did heavenly fire come down to consume Abel's but not Cain's offering (Lev. 9:24; 1 Kings 18:38)? We simply do not know. But Cain and Abel knew.

The question naturally arises as to why Jehovah accepted the one and rejected the other. Since the Bible does not say, we can only speculate. It could refer to the quality of the offerings, as we have noted. Cain chose his offering without respect to its quality or the firstfruits of his harvest. Nothing is said about his bringing the firstfruits, simply an offering (Gen. 4:3). Perhaps he kept the best for himself and gave God second-rate produce or the leftovers. On the other hand, Abel brought "the firstlings of his flock and of the fat thereof" (4:4). Fat was considered to be the choicest part of an animal. He brought the best, all of it.

All that we have belongs to God, but he permits us to use the greater part for our practical needs. However, that which we bring to him should be the best and first gift—the first and best tenth, the best of our talents and time. We should not use the best for ourselves and give the Lord the residue. To give him the *first* and *best* is an act of faith that he will provide what we need for ourselves. It is to love God above ourselves and our creature needs. We should not say that after we have satisfied our needs and luxuries we will give God what is left—if there is anything left. God has the prior claim upon us and ours. Failure to recognize this is to put self above God. And selfishness is the basis of all sin.

Furthermore, the material itself may be involved. Cain brought the fruit of the ground; Abel brought of the fruit of the flock. One brought vegetation; the other brought animal life. In Eden an apron of leaves was insufficient to cover Adam and Eve's shame. It called for skin, which implies the death of a victim. By the same token, the fruit of the ground was insufficient to cover Cain's sin. The firstling of the flock connotes animal sacrifice, the shedding of blood and life of a substitute. Later under the Mosaic Law the fruit of the ground was brought to God as a love-gift, but the blood of a substitute was required for the removal of sin. While one must not read into this scene the theological knowledge of later inspired writers, it is nevertheless eternally true, as suggested in Genesis 3:21, that "without shedding of blood is no remission" (Heb. 9:22).

On the level of spiritual understanding, without in any sense rejecting the other possibilities, the acceptance and rejection of the offering may be related to the difference in spiritual attitude of the two brothers. Their attitudes really governed the nature and material of their offerings.

Giving Cain the benefit of the doubt, let us suppose that he also brought the firstfruits of his harvest as did Abel of his flock. Each brought what he had, but evidently there was a difference, and one which both of them knew. In all likelihood, their parents had told them of their experience with the aprons of leaves and skin. If so, they both were aware of the need for sacrifice in order to cover their sin. God may even have explained the difference.

Assuming that this is true, then Cain ignored it. To be sure, he had no lamb, but he could have exchanged produce for one of Abel's lambs—a firstling. Instead, he willfully brought his produce. In this sense he was *faithless* with respect to Jehovah's demand. Like so many moderns, he did not like a bloody religion. Why not clean vegetables rather than a bloody sacrifice? On his own he provided his substitute for the *substitute*. He denied divine revelation in favor of human reason.

We may follow "the way of Cain" (Jude 11), but it leads to destruction. We may not like a *bloody religion*, preferring some more sophisticated way of salvation, but God does. And he, not us, sets the means of salvation. A way that seems right to man, but not to God, leads to death (Prov. 14:12). Only as one comes under the blood of Christ may he be accepted of God.

On the other hand, Abel followed God's will. He brought a sacrifice of the first and best of his flock. Like Abraham, he believed God, and it was accounted to him for righteousness. His was an offering of faith. He believed, not only the example of the aprons, but also the promise of Genesis 3:15. He looked forward, even beyond the sacrificial system of Israel, to the "Lamb of God, which taketh away the sin of the world" (John 1:29). Jesus called him "righteous Abel" (Matt. 23:35). He could be righteous only through the blood—not simply the blood of his lamb, but through the blood of Christ. Like Abraham, from even farther off Abel saw Messiah's day and rejoiced (John 8:56).

As Cain was *faithless,* it was by faith that Abel offered a more excellent sacrifice than that of his brother (Heb. 11:4). Even dead, he continues to speak of faith to all who would follow the Lord.

Cain also continues to speak, but quite a different message, for he was "of that wicked one" (1 John 3:12). All who heed him and follow his way are of the same. They walk in the way of unbelief or faithlessness as opposed to faith. "He that believeth on him [Christ] is not condemned [judged]: but he that believeth not is condemned [judged] already, because he hath not believed in the name of the only begotten Son of God" (John 3:18).

Fratricide

Cain's act of unbelief led to *fratricide.* John tells us that Cain, who was of that wicked one, "slew his brother." And why? "Because his own works were evil, and his brother's righteous. . . . Whosoever hateth his brother is a murderer: and ye know that no murderer hath eternal life abiding in him" (1 John 3:12, 15).

Cain was not only a murderer, but a brother-murderer. Through repentance and faith he could have been cleansed. But such was not forthcoming.

It all began when Cain brought an unacceptable offering to the Lord. Even though he had done this, God's love still sought him. God saw that Cain "was very wroth, and his countenance fell" (Gen. 4:5). Literally, "It became hot to him, and his face fell." The seething volcano on the inside showed itself in Cain's fallen face. The face of the sinner reveals his sin, deeply etched in every line. His resentment has a religious basis, and there is no fanaticism greater than that which is grounded in religious prejudice.

Cain's unacceptance before God was of his own doing, but he blamed his brother rather than himself. The sinner blames everybody but himself for his deeds. He could not stand seeing his brother enjoying God's favor while he was rejected. In a sense he was mad at society when he should have looked within himself. His was the attitude of much silly thinking today that would make society the criminal instead of the criminal himself.

But God dealt/deals with the sinner for what he was/is within himself. Asking the why of Cain's condition, God said, "If thou doest well, shalt thou not be accepted?" (4:7). We should not read into "doest well" salvation by works. Involved here is a change of heart and attitude which is the essence of repentance. Such would be followed by faith in Jehovah which would lead Cain to bring the offering fit for providing forgiveness. "Lifted up" may be seen not only as referring to his face but to his sin. Forgiveness of sin would result in a lifted countenance (Pss. 51, 32). If one shows sin in his face, he also reflects forgiveness in it.

The alternative to this is that "sin lieth [crouches] at the door" (Gen. 4:7). The figure is that of a wild beast waiting at the door to pounce upon its victim. In this case it was the harbored grudge against Abel in Cain's heart. In Cain's present mood, he was at the mercy of this beast, but God says that through repentance and faith he is to master this beast. It is one thing to be tempted, it is something else to be mastered by the temptation. Because Cain did not conquer the *beast*, he was conquered by it.

There can be no cease-fire between man and the Devil. The only way to cure a cancer is to cut it out before it spreads. The only way to deal with sin is to crush its head with the heel of him who was manifested to destroy the works of the Devil. Someone said that the way to kill a snake is to cut off its tail— just behind its ears. The serpent that ruined Cain's parents waited for him to become its third victim. Rather than destroy it, he coddled it in his bosom. And like Cleopatra and the fatal asp, it proved to be his tragic undoing.

Davies (p. 145) notes that the psychology of this event is sound, "for harboring of discontent is explosive." There is no evidence at the beginning of this story of any hostility between Cain and Abel. The hostility grew out of the situation. It was not in Abel's heart but in Cain's. Like an unremoved splinter, this resentment became infected and spread throughout his being. Had anyone prior to this occasion told Cain that he would murder his brother, he would have been horrified. But like Judas's attitude toward Jesus, what began in disappointment and frustration grew into covetousness and expressed itself full-grown in the first murder—the killing of Cain's own brother. Sin, whether it be ill will or lust, produces a terrible harvest when harbored in the heart.

> How like a mounting devil in the heart
> Rules the unrein'd ambition! Let it once
> But play the monarch, and its haughty brow
> Flows with a beauty that bewilders thought
> And unthrones peace forever. Putting on
> The very pomp of Lucifer, it turns the heart to ashes.
> —Nathanael Parker Willis

Cain's deed is a commentary on these words. Genesis 4:8

describes cold, premeditated murder. This is not so clear in the King James Version as it is in the Septuagint (the Greek translation of the Old Testament) which reads, "Let us go into the field" (RSV). While the Hebrew text does not so read, this is most likely a proper interpretation of the event. Cain lured his brother into the field, away from human habitation, where he thought his deed would hardly be discovered. There he murdered him. Murder was in his heart before it was in his hands. Pfeiffer (p. 25) notes that "of Adam's first two sons, one became a murderer, the other a martyr." Davies (p. 145) calls it "a compound of envy, hatred, and brutality." Paraphrasing Alexander Pope's words, what once had been a demon of frightful mien, seen only to be hated, was first endured, then pitied, and then embraced.

If only every man since Cain had learned from his tragic experience! What guilt and suffering would have been avoided! However, we still insist upon making our own beginnings in moral and spiritual things. Through the ages man has blundered and stumbled along, leaving a trail of human blood in his uncertain path. Hearts of hate still spawn murder. Jesus tells us that if we love rather than hate, we need have no fear of becoming murderers. Yet if one harbors hate without committing the overt act, out of lack of opportunity or fear of the consequences, he is still a murderer in his heart (Matt. 5:21–22). John echoes this truth. "Whosoever hateth his brother is a murderer" (1 John 3:15).

Cain thought that his sin was hidden. Hidden from man, but not from God, for God was quickly on the scene in judgment.

Forgotten

When I was a child my mother gave me a bucket of seed corn and told me to plant the seed in a given field. Reasoning (?) like all potential criminals I took the easy (?) way out. Instead of planting the corn, I dug a hole and poured the entire batch in and covered it up. I thought my *sin* was hidden. In due time my mother wondered why the field was not full of small corn plants. Suspicioning that something was wrong, she began to look about. To my dismay, she discovered what I had done. For true to its nature the seed had sprouted and grown up through the ground. In short order I was called to view the evidence of my sin—one small spot of ground profusely covered with small corn plants. Like Cain, I thought my sin was hidden, but you can imagine the *judgment* which soon followed. As a small boy in another field, I learned that *sin will out*.

Jehovah asked Cain, "Where is Abel thy brother?" (Gen. 4:9). God knew, but he wanted Cain to confess his sin. Instead, Cain said, "I know not." He knew all right. He knew exactly where he had buried his brother's dead body, but he lied to God. One would think that he would have confessed in bitter tears—but not so. His willful disobedience persisted. He thought he could tough it out and escape the consequences.

Then Cain asked the first question of man recorded in the Bible. "Am I my brother's keeper?" How insolent! And how prophetic! For sinful men have been asking this question ever since. It is not without design that the Holy Spirit led Moses to record this as man's first question, for it sums up man's record of inhumanity to other men. Cain was indifferent, not only to his brother's life, but to him as a person. In effect he said, "Let Abel look out for himself. I am Number One; all other people are one big zero." This attitude has turned the world into a jungle where God intended a paradise. To those unresponsive to God's love in Christ, it is the law of tooth and talon, every man for himself, and the Devil take the hindmost.

Prisoners of war released after the Vietnam War tell of the cruelty and torture inflicted upon them by people who deny the very existence of God. Those who do not recognize God have little or no regard for men. Without excusing their evil, we should also recognize the heinous nature of those who profess a recognition of God but who are still indifferent to the needs of men.

"Am I my brother's keeper?" If sin has its social aspects, so should human concern. No man is an island. We are bound up together in the bundle of life. What affects one man affects every other man. I cannot despise or harm one man without doing the same to all men. What I deny to others eventually I deny to myself. If I despise the dignity of one human personality, I deny my own. No man can be truly free until all men are free. So long as there are others who are cold, hungry, and naked, I am the same in my spirit.

Later in the story Moses says that Cain built the first city. We are living in an urban age. One can hardly deny that cities are the center of corruption and evil. Perhaps the greatest evil of all is that crowded urban centers tend to reduce an individual to less than a person. On farms and in villages people cared for each other. One man's need was every man's need—and responsibility. If a farmer's barn burned, the community came together to rebuild it.

I remember one day in the spring of 1917. My widowed mother and six of her children lived on a small farm in Alabama. As a nine-year-old, I was the only *man* on the place. Our nation was girding itself for her role in World War I. The only able-bodied men left on the farms had to do their own planting. I told my mother that I could do the plowing and get the soil ready for planting. My mother would plow the first furrow around a piece of land, called laying out the land, and then I would plow the remainder. It was slow, difficult work for me, but still there were no seeds in the ground. It was a grim picture for us.

One morning about sun-up we looked down the road. As far as we could see, wagons were coming. Our neighbors knew of the situation and had come to help out. The men plowed, the children dropped the seed in the furrows, and the women cooked the noon meal. By nightfall a forty-acre farm had been planted. These neighbors felt that they were their brother's keeper.

Perhaps the story is out of place in urban society, but it declares an ageless principle. We *are* our brother's keeper. Simply reporting a needy case to the Department of Public Welfare is not enough. This may feed hungry bodies, but it lacks the personal human touch so vital to feeding the spirit. Too often people simply look the other way, not wanting to be involved. A girl is murdered in New York City while people all about ignore her cries for help. On a cold winter night, a woman in Oklahoma City gives birth to her baby on the sidewalk. Her cries for help go unanswered by people who peer at her through the window of a warm tavern. Happily a policeman comes along, calls an ambulance, and sends mother and baby to a hospital. These stories could be duplicated almost endlessly. The fact that many people do answer such cries for help only underscores the crassness of those who do not. Am I my brother's keeper? The Bible thunders *yes!* A person or social order ignores the answer only to its detriment.

At this point Jehovah faced Cain with his sin. "What hast thou done? the voice of thy brother's blood crieth unto me from the ground" (Gen. 4:10). Cain's sin against his brother was primarily a sin against God. David recognized this fact in his sin with Bathsheba (Ps. 51:4). This is true of every sin. One may sin against his fellowman, but first, last, and always he sins against God. Atkinson (p. 60) notes that if Abel's blood cried out to God, "the clamor in the ears of God must now become unbearable." All sin calls for judgment, and that judgment is both final and temporal. Only as we confess our sin may we escape God's judgment (1 John 1:9).

As a farmer, Cain had wrested a living from the soil, but no longer. Jehovah said, "Now art thou cursed from the earth [ground], which hath opened her mouth to receive thy brother's blood from thy hand" (Gen. 4:11). Since Cain would not confess his sin, the Lord named it. Because the ground would no longer bear for him, he would be "a fugitive and a vagabond . . . in the earth" (4:12). Davies (p. 146) notes that the Kenites were Cain's descendants. They lived in Palestine as "wandering smiths, gypsies on the fringe of the field."

When Cain heard the sentence pronounced upon him, he

complained of his fate. Not one word of repentance or confession! Like Judas, he felt remorse at the outcome of his deed, but that is a far cry from godly sorrow which leads to true repentance—a change of heart, mind, and attitude. Cain had no regret as to what he had done to his brother or to God, only for what his sin had done to himself. Any occupant of death row feels as did Cain, but he is still a murderer at heart. Such an attitude is no grounds for grace, for salvation.

God showed mercy upon Cain, but would others do so? "Every one that findeth me shall slay me" (4:14). As a murderer, Cain showed no mercy, but cringed cowardly before an avenger! Nevertheless the Lord tattooed a mark on Cain to protect him. The "mark of Cain" is not that of a murderer, but of God's mercy. However, as God tempers judgment with mercy, he at times tempers mercy with judgment. This mark protected Cain, but it also insured that he would live to experience his punishment—homelessness and godlessness. The Bible does not teach soul annihilation. In hell, lost souls endure forever the second death, which is eternal separation from God. Sin separates men from both God and other men in this world, and it separates the unrepentant from God forever in hell.

So "Cain went out from the presence of the Lord, and dwelt in the land of Nod, on the east of Eden" (4:16). No one is ever out of God's *presence,* but this was Moses' way of saying that Cain left the place where he had this encounter with Jehovah, that he went away from the altar which symbolized God's presence. The lost sinner may seek to flee from God but is never out of his presence.

Nod means "wandering." It lay somewhere east of Eden, maybe east of the Caspian Sea (Dickinson, p. 62). Cain wandered, never finding a place of rest. As though trying to negate God's judgment, he built a city. The first city was built by a convicted murderer.

Cain illustrates the condition of every lost person—wandering in spiritual darkness, separated from God, ever seeking a resting place but finding none. Cain turned his back on his only hope of redemption. When he went eastward from Eden, he went away from Calvary.

A fitting close to this story may be found in the words of Donald Grey Barnhouse (vol. 1, pp. 38–39). Cain "started with human reason as opposed to divine revelation; he continued in human willfulness instead of divine will; he opposed human pride to divine humility; he sank to human hatred instead of rising by divine love; he presented human excuses instead of seeking divine grace; he went into wandering instead of seeking to return; he ended in human loneliness instead of divine fellowship. To be alone without God is the worst thing that earth can hold, to go thus into eternity is, indeed, the second death."

5

AFTER SIN COMES THE DELUGE

Genesis 6:5–9:17

WHATEVER MAY BE one's attitude toward the Bible, it is evident
that the fact of a deluge is written deeply in the mind of the
human race. Davies (p. 157) notes that approximately one
hundred stories of a great flood may be found in various parts of
the globe. In his book *The Flood Reconsidered* (p. 39) Frederick
A. Filby points out that these stories are found not only among
ancient peoples of Mesopotamia, but in China, India, Indonesia,
Ceylon, Burma, Australasia, Polynesia, among the Eskimos and
North American Indians, in Peru, Chile, and farther south. They
are found also in Greece, other European countries, Egypt and
in Central Africa. These stories appear in the folk heritage on
every continent and in the islands of the seas.

All of these, rather than being the result of spontaneous
combustion, point to a common origin. As men scattered throughout the earth they carried with them their accounts and adapted
them to their various forms of religion. Of all these stories the
Babylonian and the biblical are the most closely related. However,
the biblical is the simpler of the two. It is monotheistic in tone
as opposed to the polytheistic tone of the Babylonian. Following
the axiom of textual criticism that the simpler of two accounts
is the older and more correct, we may see the Genesis account as
the source of these many flood stories. This true story has been
augmented and embellished by various pagan people to fit their
religious beliefs.

It is not my purpose to delve into the many problems which center in the Genesis account of the flood. Such a task would require not one book but volumes. Those interested in pursuing this line of thought would do well to read Filby's work on the subject. From time to time reference will be made to this book, but at this point, to affirm my own faith in the biblical account, I quote two of Filby's conclusions. "The causes of the flood, and indeed of all great earth movements, are still largely beyond our understanding, let alone calculation. By admitting that we do not know, we leave the door wide open for further knowledge" (p. 121). In a more definite note drawn from his own search after knowledge, Filby adds, "Thus from the first statement about the Flood to the last in the book of Genesis every verse that can be questioned, examined and tried has stood the test. We have called on History, Archaeology, Geology, Radio-activity, Botany, Geography, Shipbuilding, Mythology, and Metallurgy to produce their evidence. Not one sentence of the Biblical account, carefully interpreted in its context can be shown to be incorrect or second-hand or even to be unrealistic or unlikely. It is the recorded, reliable account of an eye-witness" (p. 124).

Of course, the "eye-witness" was not Moses himself, but his source of information. This *source* does not deny or lessen divine inspiration. The Holy Spirit guided the inspired writers in the use of source material (Luke 1:1–4). The point is that in Genesis 6:5–9:17 we have the authentic account of an actual event in the history of man.

So with this brief statement we turn from the apologetic to the theological aspects of this event. And we shall center this chapter about three words: punishment, preservation, and promise.

Punishment

"And God saw that the wickedness of man was great in the earth, and that every imagination of the thoughts of his heart was only evil continually. And it repented the Lord that he had made man on the earth, and it grieved him at his heart. And the Lord said, I will destroy man whom I have created from the face of the earth; both man, and beast, and the creeping thing, and the fowls of the air; for it repenteth me that I have made them" (Gen. 6:5–7).

Man who had been created in a state of innocence had become everything but innocent. Verse 5 sums up the total departure of man from God: rebellion in Eden, murder in the field, the subsequent spread of Cain's attitude and influence. Cain did express regret over his punishment for murder, but his descendant Lamech boasted of having slain a man who wounded him, showing the progress of evil beyond Cain. Lamech's boastful attitude was utter defiance of God (4:23–24). So despite God's promise of redemption (3:15), man went his wicked way and from bad to worse.

In a sense God made a new beginning in Adam and Eve's third son Seth. "Then began men to call upon the name of the Lord" (4:26). Also "Enoch walked with God" (5:22, 24), but the general trend of mankind was away from God. This trend climaxed in the strange statement that the "sons of God" married the "daughters of men" (6:2). Whether this means that angels or angel-possessed men married human wives or that men of the line of Seth married daughters of the line of Cain (the two main interpretations), the result is a transgression of God's will. I am inclined to accept the latter interpretation. If this be true, then the *new beginning* in Seth came to a direful end. Men gave themselves to every kind of sin, not only open wickedness, but secret evil. Every imagination of their hearts was evil, not occasionally, but continually. *Imagination* to the Hebrew encompassed the whole of one's inner life. Davies (p. 151) says, "Every flight-fancy, form, fashion, imagination, impulse, purpose —of heart—mind—will is exclusively and continually evil." With the exception of Noah (and his family?), this is a picture of total depravity. Man was not sometimes good, sometimes bad— he was totally, completely, and continuously evil.

Over against the corrupt heart of man is set the *grieved* heart of God, for God was pierced to the very soul by man's evil. He who had been created in God's image and for his fellowship had become Satanic and completely unfit for God's fellowship. God's grief does not mean that he was imperfect in the joy of his own perfections. Rather God grieved because one capable of such high achievements in God's holiness had failed so miserably. Though he is transcendent, God is not unaware of or unconcerned with the earthly scene. His grief over this scene is not a mark of imperfection but of his perfection. For grief is related to love. A God who does not grieve over sin would be imperfect in his love.

Twice in Genesis 6:6–7 God is seen as repenting that he had made man. The Revised Standard Version reads that he was *sorry* that he had done so. Does this mean that God was wrong in creating man? The usual relation of repentance to wrong-doing would lead us to see error in God's creation of man. However, such a concept violates the very nature of God (see 1 Sam. 15:29). Actually the verb rendered "repented" means to take a deep breath, so to grieve or to sigh. God sighed in grief that man in his wickedness had departed so far from his purpose in creating him. How he must continue to sigh at the corruption of man even to this day!

As mysterious as it may seem to us, we are not to suppose that this depravity came as a surprise to God. In his omniscience he knows the end from the beginning. However, his foreknowledge of an event does not mean that he causes it. As seen in Genesis 3, for man to be a person he must be free. In his benevolent wisdom and power, God made even himself subject to man's response. To coerce man would be to destroy his personhood, so God rests his case upon man's response to his benevolent love. Despite man's sin, God proposed to set in operation his eternal redemptive purpose (Gen. 3:15; 4:25–26). But even Seth's line, through which God's purpose was to run, was corrupted by the line of Cain. It was necessary, therefore, to provide another line. God often changes his method but never his purpose. This change of method may also be seen in God's *repentance*.

God determined to destroy or "blot out" (RSV) man from the face of the earth or "ground" (RSV). This destruction also included beasts, creeping things, and the fowls of the air. Since this judgment would be by a flood, fish are not included.

If we are momentarily stunned by these words of judgment, at least three things should be considered. If God creates life, he also has the right to destroy it. Whether men die one by one of old age or perish en masse in a catastrophe, it is only a matter of degree. However, this mass blotting out must be seen as judgment upon evil that was beyond redemption. Indeed, God's judgment upon Noah's generation should not shock or surprise us so much as would his failure to judge so wicked a people. A holy, righteous God cannot condone or ignore evil! In a sense this judgment corresponds to the judgment of unrepentant men in hell, although the latter should not be seen as soul annihilation but as eternal punishment and separation from God. Furthermore, this judgment must be seen in the light of God's redemptive purpose. Adamic man had proved beyond doubt that this purpose could not run through him. So God proposed that it should be through Noah's line. There must be a new beginning. And this beginning called for radical surgery.

Helmut Thielicke (pp. 237 ff.) is helpful at this point. In the flood God reversed or revoked the second and third days of creation (Gen. 1:6–10). To enable life to live on earth, he divided the water surrounding the earth into an atmospheric ocean and earthly oceans with dry land on earth. But when man proved conclusively that he was beyond saving, God released the waters that he might "wash the world" to prepare it for his redemptive purpose which would not be denied.

Unlike the gods of the pagans, God did not hurl thunderbolts from some Olympus. Rather he wreaked destruction by *giving men up* to the consequences of their own evil (Rom. 1:24, 26, 28). God's grace holds in check the totally destructive power of the elements, but man in his evil reaches the point where his stubborn will shakes its clenched fist in the face of God. Then God gives him up to his own undoing. Evil sets in motion destructive forces. When evil has run its course, it brings its own retribution. "The wages of sin is death" (Rom. 6:23)! The Bible points to a second total judgment upon those who rebel finally and fully against God—not a flood of water but a flood of fire. Modern man knows only too well the destructive power locked up within the atom. God has but to give men up to their own self-willed way void of his grace, release the power which he has benevolently locked up in the atom, and then comes, not the deluge, but the holocaust.

Men presume upon the patience of God, but that patience has its extremity (Gen. 6:3). The time comes when God says, "It is enough!" Then comes the catastrophe. Thielicke (p. 239) comments:

> So the descent goes on and on. Corruption spreads like a prairie fire—and then the mighty force of the Flood breaks in upon it.
>
> It's always the same old story: because man does what is unholy, he provokes the floods of damned-up mischief. Because he no longer wants to live by grace, the dams which are held up by grace are broken.

Preservation

The story of the flood also speaks of *preservation*. Immediately following the statement of God's purpose to punish evil men, Moses adds, "But Noah found grace in the eyes of the Lord" (Gen. 6:8). He was excepted from the general destruction which was to come. He and his family of eight were to be spared. Through them, God proposed to make a new beginning for mankind, not only for the preservation of the race, but for the working of God's redemptive purpose. As in Eden so here; in the midst of judgment is presented the hope of redemption from sin.

Noah found grace, not on the basis of his merit, but on the basis of God's love and purpose. Though Noah was himself a sinful creature, he was not identified with the totally corrupt order in which he lived. In him were the qualities which God could use in his eternal purpose. It was a case of "Jacob have I loved, but Esau have I hated" (Rom. 9:13; see Mal. 1:2–3). This refers not to God's emotions but to his choice. "Noah was a righteous man, blameless in his generation; Noah walked with God" (Gen. 6:9, RSV). Noah was not perfect but a man whom God could use (9:21). W. O. Carver once said, "God has no perfect individuals or institutions through which to work. He has to get along with us just the way we are the best he can." Noah was such a man.

Even the best of Christians is but a sinner saved by grace, a grace made possible through the redemptive work of Christ. As we look back to that event in faith, so Noah looked forward in faith in God's redemptive promise (3:15). Like Abraham, he saw Messiah's day and rejoiced.

Noah's righteousness is all the more remarkable since he lived in such a corrupt social order—which testifies to the fact that a lily may grow in a cesspool. Even this was the fruit of God's grace. There is saving grace, but there is also enabling grace. Whatever good men may do is by the grace of God. The best of them can only say with Paul, "By the grace of God I am what I am" (1 Cor. 15:10).

In order that God might preserve a remnant, he told Noah to build an ark. This was one hundred and twenty years before the flood (Gen. 6:3). The ark was to be made of "gopher wood" (6:14). The word *gopher* appears nowhere else in the Bible, and its meaning is uncertain. Even Brown, Driver, and Briggs in their Hebrew lexicon say that they have no idea of the origin of the word. They suggest "pitch-wood" or "resin-wood." Since the Phoenicians used cypress for ship building due to its lightness and strength, this probably was the wood used. To make it water-tight, the ark was to be covered inside and out with "pitch," a material which abounded in the area, evidence of the oil deposits which are so plentiful there today.

The size of the ark according to modern measurements, figuring a cubit as 18 inches, was 75 feet wide, 45 feet high, and 450 feet long. Filby (p. 93) compares this to some of the great ocean liners of the modern era and it corresponds favorably to them in ratio. Some critics insist that this was too great an undertaking for ancient man. Filby (p. 92) answers by citing such gigantic feats as the Great Pyramid built long before Abraham, the Colossi of Memnon, and the Colossus of Rhodes. Granted that the building of the ark antedates these, they show that ancient man was capable of large construction and of exact engineering skill.

I am reminded of two tall columns at the temple of Luxor in Egypt. They were erected at a time which generally corresponds to the time of Moses. These columns stand erect with nothing to fasten them to their base, yet through more than thirty centuries they have stood, resisting wind and weather. One marvels at the exact engineering skill involved in their building. Modern man would do well to remember that wisdom was not born with him. Indeed, modern engineering rests upon principles which date from antiquity, principles which were wrought out by pure mental power without the aid of modern mechanical devices. When we recall these things, plus the wisdom of God involved, there is no reasonable basis on which to question Noah's ability to build the ark. And he had one hundred and twenty years to do it!

The author of Hebrews says that "by faith Noah, being warned of God of things not seen as yet . . . prepared an ark to the saving of his house; by which he condemned [judged guilty] the world, and became heir of the righteousness which is by faith" (Heb. 11:7).

Why, indeed, build an ark? A small boat to sail on the river, perhaps, but so large a ship in a dry land so far from the sea? Surely it was madness! So must have thought Noah's contemporaries. It takes little imagination to see Noah and his sons working amid the jeers of the crowd. They must have laughed with scorn when the patriarch warned of a flood—when there was not a single cloud in the sky. Peter speaks of the longsuffering of God in the days of Noah (1 Pet. 3:20). But this longsuffering was to no avail, for rather than repenting the people sinned more and more. Even if God had spoken to Noah, as he claimed, they virtually dared God to fulfill his word.

Paul described such people in Romans 2:2–5. "But we are sure that the judgment of God is according to truth against them which commit such things. And thinkest thou this, O man, . . . that thou shalt escape the judgment of God? Or despisest thou the riches of his goodness and forbearance and longsuffering; not knowing that the goodness of God leadeth thee to repentance? But after thy hardness and impenitent heart treasurest up unto thyself wrath against the day of wrath and revelation of the righteous judgment of God." Paul's question might well be directed to modern man who defies God and ignores the warning signs of our day which point to destruction.

Finally the ark was finished. At God's direction, certain animal life was placed in the ark for preservation. God told Noah and his family to enter. Then "the Lord shut him in" (Gen. 7:16). Judgment time had come! While those outside the ark were soon to be destroyed, Noah and his family were safe, not by any act of their own other than faith in and obedience to God's word. God shut them in from the destruction about to fall upon the earth and its totally depraved people.

The flood came, but not simply by rain in the normal sense. "The fountains of the great deep [were] broken up, and the windows of heaven were opened" (7:11). The *deep* refers to the ocean. This suggests that upheavals in the earth brought about the breaking up of the bounds of the oceans. This was accompanied by atmospheric disturbances causing continuous torrential rain. Davies (p. 155) describes it:

> The method of destruction is by a flood of water by which is meant not rain or inundation in the normal sense, but the

cosmic ocean which is above the firmament (1:7), and beneath the earth. The Hebrew word for flood is used only of Noah's flood and occurs 12 times in chapters 6–9. This cosmic ocean floods the earth through the opened windows of the firmament, and the springs in the ground, through which the waters well up (7:11).

In either case the earth was covered with water. Again Davies notes, "So vast was the deluge of waters that the whole world was drowned, even the highest mountains were about 28 feet below the surface, and all life—men and beasts—was obliter-ated" (p. 155; Gen. 7:19–22). On this point Davies cites John Bright and Charles F. Pfeiffer (p. 31) and suggests that the flood resulted from "heavy rains from above, and the 'fountains of the deep' from beneath. The latter may refer to earthquakes with accompanying tidal waves. Volcanic eruptions suddenly raising the ocean floor and the fall of giant meteorites into the sea are also suggested." But however one may explain it, there is no reason to question the fact of Scripture which is supported by archeological and geological evidence (see Filby, chapter 1).

Even if one accepts the objections raised by some to a universal flood, this does not contradict the biblical record. In his work Filby (pp. 82–83) shows that the various uses of the Hebrew word for "earth" allow for a flood which was either universal or confined to the Mesopotamian Valley. It could mean the entire earth or all of a portion of it. The latter does not necessarily mean a concession to modern geology. "It may be well to point out that Matthew Poole in his *Synopsis* (1670) and Bishop Edward Stillingfleet (1662), both held that the Bible did not necessitate a belief that the Flood covered the entire planet. These books were written 180 years before the real development of modern geology" (Filby, p. 84).

In all candidness, the whole "earth" as Noah knew it satisfies the demands of the biblical narrative. One must not tell God how he did it, but must accept the Genesis account in keeping with the elasticity of the Hebrew word for *earth*. If God proposed to flood the entire planet, he had the power to do it. His purpose was to destroy wicked man. The Bible itself shows that at the time of the flood man was still confined to the Mesopotamian Valley (Gen. 11:9).

We should not become so embroiled in debate over the extent of the flood that we lose the fact and purpose of it. The Bible says that such a flood took place. Even the records of pagan people point to the fact of it. The Bible says that it was for judgment upon sin and that in judgment God showed mercy toward Noah and his family.

Neither should we miss the larger lesson involved in the Old Testament event. It points to the greater mercy which God shows to all who believe in Christ, for the ark is a type of Christ. As all in the ark were saved from God's judgment through the flood, so all who are in Christ are saved from God's judgment upon sin —even the final judgment upon Satan and all evil forces. "Whosoever believeth in him should not perish, but have eternal life" (John 3:16, ASV).

Peter speaks of Christ's redeeming work in terms of the saving of Noah and his family in the ark. "While the ark was a preparing, wherein few, that is, eight souls were saved by [*dia*, through] water. The like figure [antitype] whereunto even baptism doth also now save us . . . by the resurrection of Jesus Christ" (1 Pet. 3:20–21). Some see this as teaching baptismal regeneration. But the word rendered "baptism" (*baptisma*) refers, not to the act of baptism (*baptismos*), but to the meaning in the act, namely, the death, burial, and resurrection of Jesus Christ. Noah and his family were not saved by being in the water; they were saved *through* the water or flood by being in the ark. Outside the ark they would have perished; inside the ark they were safe. Likewise, outside of Christ we are lost. But if we are *in Christ* we are both saved and safe. Baptism symbolizes that which we trust for salvation—the death, burial, and resurrection of Christ. It also symbolizes our own death to sin, our burial, and our resurrection to a new life in Christ. Furthermore baptism symbolizes faith in the final resurrection of our body at the Lord's return (Rom. 6:3–5).

Therefore, as Noah and his family were saved from God's judgment of sin in their day, so in Christ we are not under God's judgment now. Neither will we come under his final judgment (John 3:16–18). A sinful and condemned world may scoff at our faith, but in the time of judgment they will be condemned, and we will be vindicated and glorified. This is the assurance that is in us, an assurance of which the world knows nothing. It may seem as foolishness to those who are perishing, but it is. the power and wisdom of God unto salvation to all who through faith in God's true Ark are being saved (1 Cor. 1:18–25).

Promise

One year and ten days after the flood began, Noah stepped out of the ark onto dry ground (Gen. 7:11; 8:13–14). The first thing he did was to erect an altar and offer burnt offerings unto God (8:20). Probably the last words Jehovah heard as he shut the door of the ark were the cursings and jeerings of sinful men. Though the actual words are not recorded, we may well imagine that the first ones spoken by Noah after leaving the ark were those of praise and thanksgiving in worship. God had truly washed the world. In this context we read of his promise never again to judge the earth and its inhabitants through a flood (8:21–22). The mention of the order of the seasons in verse 22 suggests that they had been disturbed in a cataclysmic judgment. This will never happen again. Individual sin will be judged, to be sure, but such a mass judgment will not come again "while the earth remaineth" (8:22). The next great judgment corresponding to the flood will be one of fire at the end of the age (2 Pet. 3:6–11). Thielicke (p. 235) treats the two cataclysmic judgments of God upon rebellious men under the heading "Floods and Fires."

While God did not promise that he would not again judge the world in catastrophic form, he did promise that he would not do so through a flood. This is the promise to the new humanity which descends from Noah. Davies (p. 156) calls the covenant with Noah "unilateral," for no obligation is placed upon Noah. God simply gives his promise.

As a token or sign of God's faithfulness, he said, "I do set my bow in the cloud" (see Gen. 9:13, 14, 16). Elsewhere in the Old Testament this Hebrew word is used for a military bow; with its bowstring drawn back it is an instrument of destruction. But in this context the bowstring is flat on the ground with the multicolored bow arched above it, showing that in the present storm event God is not bent upon destruction. This bow symbolizes God's protection in the storm. Forever thereafter during his life we may imagine that every time storm clouds gathered, Noah's heart would tremble as he remembered the flood. But when the rainbow appeared, he would be reminded that God remembers his covenant, and then his heart would be at peace.

The rainbow has become a symbol of God's protection over his people in life's storms. Twice the word *rainbow* is used in the Bible (Rev. 4:3; 10:1). Revelation was written to Christians undergoing severe Roman persecution under Domitian. Perhaps they were wondering if Satan had dethroned God. Was it worthwhile to be faithful to Christ? If God was dethroned and Satan reigned, there was no hope. To encourage them, John was given a view of heaven. There he saw God seated on his throne. "A throne was set in heaven, and one sat on the throne." The Greek verb translated "was set" is in a tense which shows continuous action in past time. There never had been a time when the throne was not there, and the one sitting on the throne was not Satan or Caesar, but God. Despite the persecution of his people on earth, God was still in control. "And there was a rainbow round about the throne." Here the rainbow symbolizes God's protection over his people. In Revelation 10:1 an angel is pictured as having a rainbow upon his head. Some see this angel as

Christ. I see him as the angel of the vindication of the saints or the people of God. In both instances the rainbow suggests God's protection of his own.

It is significant that the rainbow was "round about" the throne. It encircled the throne. On the ground a rainbow appears as a half-circle. When seen from space, it is a full circle, which suggests that the view in Revelation 4:3 is from heaven. On earth men may think that all is lost, but at such a time they should look up, not about. Doing so in faith they can know that God is fully aware of the situation and that his token of promise encircles him.

The promise made to Noah still stands—no more earth-destroying, race-destroying floods. Even when billows of trouble seem to overwhelm us, we can look up and see the rainbow encircling the throne of God. He not only rules the universe but also cares for the least of his children. Amid toil and tribulation we hear the voice of our blessed Savior saying, "Be of good cheer [courage]; I have overcome [fully conquered] the world" (John 16:33).

However, we should not let the promise given to Noah lull us into complacency. Although God has promised never again to destroy the world by water, he also has said that the moment will come when the present order will be destroyed by fire. The passage in 2 Peter 3:2–11 is but one of many to this effect. Then, as now, scoffers deny that it will happen, but Peter reminds us that as the flood came, so will the fire. Time is no element with God, but he keeps his promises. His delay is to the end that men shall have opportunity to repent of sin and find life in his Son. However, as in the days of Noah, life will go its normal way until finally God will say, "It is enough!" Then as with the cosmic and earthly seas, he will withdraw his grace from restraining the power bound up in the atom. "The day of the Lord will come as a thief in the night; in the which the heavens shall pass away with a great noise, and the elements shall melt with fervent heat, the earth also and the works that are therein shall be burned up" (2 Pet. 3:10). In the light of the nuclear age, wise men no longer scoff or regard Peter's words as mere ancient imagery. His words should sober everyone into serious reflection and positive action.

"Seeing then that all these things shall be dissolved, what manner of persons ought ye to be in all holy conversation and godliness" (2 Pet. 3:11)? Your "conversation" or manner of life should be one of preparedness and constant expectation. You should be in Christ, the Ark prepared for your salvation, and busy about the work of the Lord. For at some split second of time known only to God, he will shut the door of his Ark. All within shall be safe; all outside will be without hope.

The Book of Revelation contains three series of sevens: seals, trumpets, and bowls. Each deals with God's judgment upon evil. Each presents the progressive nature of this judgment. But when men refused to repent as the result of the seal and trumpet judgments, as the complete judgment of the bowls is anticipated, an angel of God says, "There should be time no longer" (Rev. 10:6). The sense of this is that there will be no more delay. After temporal judgments are ignored, complete, final judgment comes without delay.

What does this say to us? The temporal judgments which abound on every hand today are designed to bring us to repentance and faith in Jesus Christ. But it is evident that rather than repent, in the large man plunges deeper and deeper into sin. God's delay in final judgment should not be construed as his indifference or unending patience. Rather it is an expression of his grace. As in Noah's day, so in ours, the time will come as a thief in the night—when least expected—when God will unleash the destructive powers of his creation. Then comes the holocaust—not flood but fire. Those in the Ark of Christ need have no fear, but for those who have rejected him there will be no hope.

To the wicked in Noah's day the flood was a catastrophe, but to Noah it was a confirmation of his faith. So will it be with the *fire*. The wicked will seek a hiding place, but find none. For the saints of God it will be a welcomed vindication and will usher in everlasting peace. While the storms of life rage, the Christian may look up and see the encircling rainbow about him who sits on the throne of the universe. And in this assurance he finds rest.

> Serene I fold my hands and wait,
> Nor care for wind or tide or sea;
> I rave no more 'gainst time or fate
> For lo! my own shall come to me.
>
> Serene I fold my hands and wait,
> Whate'er the storms of life may be.
> Faith guides me up to Heaven's gate
> And Love will bring my own to me.
> —JOHN BURROUGHS.*

---

*Quoted in Virginia Ely, *I Quote* (New York: Stewart, 1947), pp. 247–48.

6

REACHING FOR THE STARS

Genesis 11:1–9

SEVERAL YEARS AGO I was interviewed by a news reporter in Porte Alegre, Brazil. It was early in the Space Age. He asked me what I thought about the claim of some that probing into space is sinful. I replied that in my judgment the probing itself is not sinful. The possibility of sins lies in what men do with what they learn. Under God man is to have dominion. If someone notes that this dominion was limited to things in the sea, air, and on the earth, it may just as well be applied to earth, sea, and sky. Man's first capabilities limited him to this planet; his ingenuity now enables him to reach for the stars. The dominion is one of degree; wresting from nature her secrets and treasures by digging a well, drilling for oil, mining for minerals, and probing into space. To abuse dominion is sin; to use it for man's good and God's glory is spiritual service.

In his present effort to reach for the stars, man would be wise to profit by the ancient experience connected with the building of the Tower of Babel, for the principles set forth there are of universal application. Genesis 10 lists the descendants of Noah's sons Shem, Ham, and Japeth, and the areas of the earth to which they eventually migrated. Genesis 11:1–9 relates the reason for this migration.

Pride

One of man's besetting sins is *pride*. "For all that is in the world, the lust of the flesh, and the lust of the eyes, and the pride of life, is not of the Father, but is of the world" (1 John 2:16). One would think that man at this early stage, recalling the flood, would be everything but a creature of pride. Even more, that we, reviewing the tragic fruits of such behavior would be humble before God. However, such is not the case, for the heart of natural man is exceedingly wicked. Proverbs 6:18 says that the Lord hates "an heart that deviseth wicked imaginations, feet that be swift in running to mischief."

According to Genesis 10:25 the earth was divided in the days of Peleg. In Hebrew the name *Peleg* means "division." In 11:1–9 Moses relates how this division took place.

"The whole earth was of one language, and of one speech" (11:1). The "whole earth" here apparently refers to the Mesopotamian Valley in which all of mankind dwelt at this time. The Hebrew word for *language* means "lip." *Speech* literally means "words." It is possible that the former refers to lips sounds or phonetics, and the latter to vocabulary. The Revised Standard Version renders this "one language and few words."

As limited as the vocabulary may have been, it was a means of communication which contributed to unity. Language is of vital importance in human history. Man alone has the power of speech, one of the major differences between him and animals. Someone has noted that animals' cries express emotion and arouse emotions in other animals, but they do not convey thought or reason. By language men transmit the thoughts of their minds. And, whereas similarity of language promotes unity, a difference of language tends toward separation. For instance, the Greeks called non-Greek-speaking people Barbarians. To them any other language sounded like "bar bar." Even today, unless there are other causes of division, people who speak the same tongue feel an unusual bond of unity with one another. On the other hand, people tend to fear that which is strange, whether it be culture or language. The sound of one's own tongue in a foreign country is sweet music to a traveler's ears.

The united descendants of Noah were a migratory people. Traveling from the east toward the west, they came to a plain in Shinar (the ancient name for Mesopotamia), and there they dwelt or "settled" (11:2, rsv). Since they did not propose to continue wandering, they proceeded to build permanent habitations by agreeing to make burnt brick. Moses notes that they used these "brick for stone, and slime [bitumen, rsv] . . . for mortar" (11:3). This reflects the language of one familiar with Palestine where the normal building material was stone which abounded there. One interpreter makes a point out of the fact that they used artificial building material (bricks) rather than stones which God had made. He says that these early people unknowingly depicted the attitude of sinners in substituting the artificial for the natural. While this latter is true, it hardly is the meaning of this verse. They simply used what was at hand. That which constitutes evil in this case was not the building material itself but the purpose of heart which lay behind the enterprise. However, it is true that Jesus said that one who does not build upon his word and will is building upon a foundation of sand. He who builds his life in keeping with Jesus' words and will is building upon a rock. When the storms of life come the former falls, while the latter endures.

The sinful purpose in this experience is expressed in 11:4. "Let us build us a city and a tower, whose top may reach unto heaven; and let us make us a name, lest we be scattered abroad upon the face of the whole earth." Note the threefold use of "let us" in verses 3–4. Their purpose was centered in their own egotism, with no recognition of God. Rather than saying, "Thy will be done," they said, "Let us do our will." They proposed to build "us" a city and tower and to make "us" a name. God had no part in it. It was not for his glory but for man's glory. The purpose was to preserve their unity lest they be scattered over the entire earth; so as a rallying point they proposed to build a tower which would reach unto heaven. The Revised Standard Version reads "a tower with its top in the heavens."

Several things are suggested by this verse. First, the unity which they enjoyed was not as stable as one might imagine. It was based upon a oneness of language rather than upon a spiritual kinship wrought by their worship of the one true God. In a sense it was an outward union rather than a spiritual unity. A family or nation held together by externals, such as material possessions or political or even military power, is resting on shifting sand. The only union worthwhile is born out of spiritual qualities, aims, and ideals. "Except the Lord build the house, they labour in vain that build it: except the Lord keep the city, the watchman waketh but in vain" (Ps. 127:1).

It is of interest that they built a city. The first city was built by a murderer (Gen. 4:17). It is hardly any surprise, therefore, that cities are centers of corruption and crime. When I was a boy living on a farm, we never locked the doors of the barn or the house. But in most any major city in America today, hotel rooms abound in signs telling the occupants to lock the door, even to use the safety chain lock. In many such cities people are warned not to be out on the streets after dark. Cities like this, rather than unifying people, divide them into predatory animals and their prey. Even where this is not true, the crowding of people into cities tends to reduce them to less than persons. They become statistics. People often witness crimes, even murder, with hardly a protest, simply because they do not want to be involved.

I shall never forget a story told to me by a relative who had lived in New York City for twenty-five years and drove a city bus. Across the hall in his apartment house lived another bus driver. To enable the drivers to get their buses in service for the morning rush, the company ran an early bus to pick up the drivers. Almost every morning for twenty-five years these two drivers met in the hall and walked two blocks to the bus line. Not once in all these years did they so much as say "Good morning" to each other. No, cities do not unite, they divide.

Furthermore, this city was built upon selfish egotism. "Let us make us a name." God was not in it, only man. Their effort represents an early type of *humanism*. In a sense these people worshiped man and his prowess—the predominant religion of today. In this age of scientific and technological achievements man tends to deify himself. Men say, "We have done great things today; we will do greater things tomorrow." The result is a big man and a little God—in man's concept.

This is the sense in which the Bible uses the term *world* as opposed to a spiritual outlook on life. The *world* represents a social order built upon man's ability, with little or no recognition of God. We ignore the divine standards of conduct and set up those of our own making; everything becomes relative. Righteousness is measured, not by the nature of God, but by the whims of man. God himself is limited to man's ability. What man does not know and cannot do is denied to God. Man becomes the captain of his soul and the master of his fate. With God's standards scuttled, man becomes rudderless, adrift on the sea of time. It is no wonder that he is caught up in confusion and frustration.

However, the center of this story is the tower which was supposed to reach up to the heavens. Donald Grey Barnhouse (vol. 1, p. 71) questions the idea that the tower was to reach up to heaven itself. "They would be doubly fools to start it by a river when there were mountains in sight a few miles away that would have given them a great start." It is possible to see this phrase as hyperbole (Deut. 1:28), but obviously the idea is that of a tower of great height. Atkinson (p. 108) sees this as a tall tower with a dome resembling the dome of heaven. Inside this dome were painted the signs of the zodiac. From this height the priests hoped to secure knowledge of the stars, which suggests idolatrous worship. Atkinson comments, "It seems likely that the intention was to establish a centre of heathen religion." "It was an open, defiant turning to Satan and the beginning of devil worship. This is why the Bible everywhere pronounces a curse on those who consult the sun, the moon, and the stars of heaven" (Barnhouse, p. 71). This story sounds a warning to an age which has gone wild in its absorbing interest in the occult, astrology, horoscopes, and related matters.

It should be noted, however, that there is a vast difference between these things and space exploration. Rather than to worship the heavenly bodies, the purpose of the space program is to *subdue* the planets that they may serve the purposes of men.

Several years ago I heard the late President Lyndon B. Johnson (then vice-president) explain one of this nation's goals in space exploration. He pointed out that prior to World War I the nation which controlled the seas controlled the world (England). Since that time the nation which controlled the skies controlled the world (United States). Then he added that in the future the nation which controls space will control the world. It will be far better for a nation which subscribes to Christian principles to be that nation than one which denies the existence of God altogether.

Even if one takes the words "unto heaven" literally, the tower represents man's efforts to achieve his salvation through his own efforts. The Hebrew word rendered "Babel" means "the gate of God." It was associated with the Hebrew letters *bll*, so that, by a play on words, it came to denote confusion (Gen. 11:9). Man in his pride proposed to climb up to the gate of God by his own power, with no reliance upon God.

Among the ruins of ancient Babylon is a temple-tower, or ziggurat, which is called Etemenanki, "the House of the Terrace-platform of Heaven and Earth." Charles F. Pfeiffer (p. 37) says, "It is possible that the unfinished Tower of Babel was put to use in the building of this ziggurat which dominated the sky line of Babylon in a later day." To say the least, it stands as a reminder of ancient man's prideful effort to build a civilization without recognition of and in rebellion against God. And it speaks of such futile efforts down the ages—even today.

The root sin is selfishness—centering life in self rather than in God. Any system of endeavor or religion which does this is of the Devil. The entire story of the proposal to build the Tower of

Babel reeks with defiance of God. However, one does not have to shake his clenched fist in God's face to rebel against him. It may be done by denying his existence, ignoring him, or by paying him lip-service while pursuing one's own worldly goals and ideals. While all three of these are found in various segments of today's society, the last is the most prevalent. The troubles which assail us on every hand largely stem from this attitude. God has his own redemptive plan by which to unify men, and they ignore it to their own self-destruction. Pride of achieve-ment is equaled by inordinate pride which prevents us from confessing our sins—personal and social—and receiving God's forgiveness. The very patience of God restrains his judgment, but man mistakenly interprets this as God's indifference toward evil and/or his impotence to act on behalf of righteousness. This serves only to increase man's selfish pride and self-reliance.

In such a state we would do well to read prayerfully Psalm 2: "Why do the heathen rage, and the people imagine a vain thing? The kings of the earth set themselves, and the rulers take counsel together, against the Lord, and against his anointed, saying, Let us break their bands asunder, and cast away their cords from us. He that sitteth in the heavens shall laugh: the Lord shall have them in derision. Then shall he speak unto them in his wrath, and vex them in his sore displeasure. Yet have I set my king upon my holy hill of Zion. . . . Kiss the Son, lest he be angry, and ye perish from the way, when his wrath is kindled but a little. Blessed are all they that put their trust in him."

Pettiness

Penitence, not pride, is the crying need of this hour! If it does not come voluntarily, it will come as the fruit of divine judgment upon a people or person who in pride turns up the nose to God.

This passage from the psalms suggests that despite man's pride in his achievements, they are all *pettiness* to God. This thought is further suggested by Genesis 11:5. "And the Lord came down to see the city and the tower, which the children of men builded." Obviously this is an anthropomorphism. It pictures God acting as a man, the ancient's way of introducing God's intervention to thwart this defiant proposal of man. However, from it we may see certain evident theological truths.

For one thing, God is mindful of the ways of men. The Bible knows nothing of a deistic God who created the universe, set it in motion as a giant machine, and then went off and left it to grind on impersonally. God is concerned about his universe and about man. He is in the universe but not contained by it. Because he is present in it, he is concerned about it, and his primary concern centers in man.

God did not need to come down on an inspection tour in order to learn what man was doing. Omniscient, he knows all things simultaneously. He that sits in the heavens knew what man was doing and why he was doing it. Genesis 11:5 was Moses' way of saying that God involved himself in this prideful affair.

Although God knew that another judgment of man was necessary, he did not bring it about arbitrarily. His judgments are true and righteous (Rev. 16:7). Using human language, God inspected the evidence before reaching a verdict. This was true in Eden and in Noah's day, and it is true on the plain of Shinar. God waited until the tower was completed; in a sense man was caught with his hand in the cookie jar. When God judges there is no excuse available to man.

However, the most picturesque truth in this verse is that God "came down" to see the tower which man had built. Prideful man was going to build a tower that reached up to heaven, but when he had exhausted all his engineering skill, still God had to *come down* to see it. It fell far short of man's lofty and worldly ambition. What seemed to be so great in the eyes of man was petty indeed in the eyes of God.

Visiting Yosemite National Park a number of years ago, we

were enraptured by the giant waterfalls and the mountains which seemed to reach the sky. Recently as I flew over this area the pilot pointed out the park. From our altitude it was insignificant indeed. This expresses somewhat God's view of man's tower.

Recently a newspaper article reported that astronomers at the University of California, using the 120-inch telescope at the Lick Observatory, had discovered a new quasar (quasi-stellar object). They believe it is ten billion light-years away from the earth. This quasar called OQ–172 is some fifty million light-years farther away than the previously discovered most distant object OH–471. It astounds one to think that the light which was so recently seen left this quasar ten billion light-years ago!

All of which serves to show how petty are modern man's achievements when compared with the omnipotence and omniscience of God as revealed in his seemingly boundless universe. Rather than being elated with pride, we should be humbled before God as we fall on our faces before him, crying, "How great thou art!"

The more man learns as he reaches for the stars, the greater should be his comprehension of the glory of Christ. These ancient tower builders, in a sense, sought to center the universe in themselves—the very essence of sin. We should learn from the greatness of the universe how great is Christ, who holds it all together (Col. 1:17).

Christ gives order to the universe; likewise, order in a society or in a person is to be found only in complete devotion to him. Men would do well to remember that when they have achieved their highest potential in the natural order they are not gods but pygmies before the infinite greatness of Christ. Unity of person or nations is to be found only in a right spiritual relation to him. So long as we insist upon building our own petty towers as the "gate of God," so long will we be plagued with frustration and strife, for God still *comes down* to confuse such efforts.

The grand note of the gospel is that in Christ, God *came down* to become Jesus of Nazareth, completely identifying himself with us apart from sin. In his redeeming work he opened the "gate of God" that all who receive his Son as Savior may become children of God—"heirs of God, and joint-heirs with Christ" (Rom. 8:17) of all that God is and has.

Uncounted years after the event at Babel, Jacob in a dream saw a ladder reaching from earth to heaven, with the angels of God ascending and descending upon it (Gen. 28:12). Jesus told Nathanael that he is the true ladder into heaven (John 1:51). It is, therefore, in him whose name is above every name (Phil. 2:9) that we may make a *name* for ourselves (Christian) and by whom we may walk through the true gates of God into eternal life, unity, and glory. We shall do this, not in prideful endeavor, but in humble submission as we see the pettiness of our own achievements and the glory of God's redemptive grace and love as revealed in Christ Jesus. Rather than to attempt, we must *submit* in faith to him who alone is the Way, the Truth, and the Life.

Punishment

Because these ancients did not submit, they received God's *punishment*. The Lord's inspection tour confirmed their rebellious purpose. With the tower completed, they would now proceed to build a city. Rather than replenishing the earth, they would remain about their pagan shrine; so God proceeded to confound their proposal. One might expect an earthquake to topple the tower to the ground, or a rain of fire to destroy the people. But not so. God worked a miracle within their brains and vocal cords (Barnhouse, vol. 1, p. 72), so that their language was confounded or confused. The one thing which had united them now drove them apart (Gen. 11:7–8), and they "left off to build the city."

Since they could no longer understand one another's speech, the workmen could not comprehend the utterances of the overseers. Confusion reigned, and in desperation they abandoned the project. Gradually those who could understand one another came together, and these groups then wandered off in different directions. In time they scattered over the earth (Gen. 10).

Some interpreters explain the difference of language by noting the people's separation, but the Bible says the opposite. It was not a gradual growth from different dialects to various languages; it was an instant miracle of God. It is true that linguists can trace the development and source of different languages, for instance, the Romance languages from the Latin, but this was a subsequent development. Linguists have found certain links between a few of the most ancient languages, suggesting that originally these were derived from the same source in the distant, unrecorded past. The Bible does record that of which other known historical records are silent.

This confusion of tongues may be seen as related to God's redemptive purpose (see Atkinson, p. 109; Davies p. 166). This is strangely true. At Babel, man's purpose was to build a civilization with no recognition of God. Had he succeeded in his proud purpose, man could not have been restrained in his evil aim. But God lets men go only so far in their wicked designs. There comes a time when he says, "It is enough." He said it in his judgments in Eden and in Noah's day, and he repeated it at Babel. History records events which secular historians attribute to various natural, political, economical, military, and cultural causes, but the sacred historian sees the hand of God at work— frustrating men's evil purposes, and within it all guiding events toward his eternal redemptive purpose. God does not cause the wicked doings of men, but he works in all things to overrule them as he guides history toward his intended goal.

In Romans 1 Paul notes that as men scattered they carried their paganism with them. But still God did not leave himself without a witness. He continued to make himself known in nature, in the pagan conscience, and through his more direct revelation to those who at least in measure acknowledged him (Rom. 1–2). His witness occurred even as men's paganism led them into blind alleys of frustration and ruin. In the fullness of time, the time of God's own choosing, he sent forth his Son to provide redemption for all who would believe in him (Gal. 4:4–5). Thus we see that even God's punishment at Babel had an ultimate benevolent end.

One cannot fail to relate the confusion of tongues at Babel to the miracle of tongues at Pentecost. As by a miracle he divided men in the confusion of languages in the former, so in the latter by another miracle, he enabled his evangels to speak languages other than their own, that men of other tongues and dialects might hear and believe the gospel of redemption. Through the Christian centuries, those devoted to God's call have submitted to the discipline of language study that men of other tongues might hear the gospel in their own languages. The fruit of such has been a unity based, not upon a oneness of speech, but upon a oneness of faith and love.

Many times in my life I have been thrown with people who spoke my own tongue, but the foul vocabulary they used made any unity of spirit impossible. At other times I have been with people whose language I did not know, but as they sang and preached the gospel I felt a spiritual oneness with them which transcended outward differences of language, culture, nation, or other diverse interests.

I shall never forget a day spent in Cairo, Egypt, in 1955. Our touring party was made up of strangers in a strange land. We were a little island of America in an ocean of another world. Our very dress separated us from them. We were committed to entirely different economic and political systems. We were Christians, and they were Muslims. All day long we had heard them pray, trade, haggle, fight, and curse each other in Arabic, not a word of which we understood.

Finally, that evening we found ourselves in a small Baptist church located on a back street of that teeming city. The differences of language, culture, and political persuasion were still evident. The outward difference from what we had seen all day was evidenced by clean, well-mannered children, smiles, and hearty handshakes. There was no begging for alms, but a giving of love and goodwill.

When the worship service began, we were welcomed, not as tourists, but as brethren in Christ. Finally, we began to sing—we in English and they in Arabic. The song was "Amazing Grace." We could not understand one another's words, but we felt one another's spirits in love for Christ and for one another. For the first time in my life I knew what a difference Christ makes.

Since that time I have had similar experiences in Japan, Korea, Taiwan, Hong Kong, India, Africa, Europe, Russia, the Middle East, Latin America, and the islands of the seas. The sense of oneness in Christian love has been felt in each place.

The Baptist World Alliance is a fellowship of more than thirty million Baptists from every part of the globe. Every five years thousands of them meet in a Baptist World Congress. In 1965 this congress met in Miami Beach, Florida. A unity of fellowship was evident on every hand. The president elected for the next five years was Dr. William R. Tolbert, Jr., then vice-president but now president of Liberia, West Africa. He was the first black man to be chosen for this office, and he was elected without a single discordant note.

Since I was chosen as the North American vice-president, I was present in the press conference which followed Dr. Tolbert's election. One reporter, noting that the Baptists over the earth spoke many different languages, asked him how many languages he spoke. He replied, "Only English."

"How then," asked the reporter, "will you communicate with them?"

"I will speak to them in the language of love," Dr. Tolbert replied.

Yes, the universal language of Christian love. For Christ has broken down the middle wall of partition, making in himself one new man, so making peace (Eph. 2:14–15). Reconciled to God, men become reconciled to one another. We may know the unity of the Spirit in the bond of peace (Eph. 4:3), and thus Babel is transformed into united songs of praise.

> People and realms of ev'ry tongue
> Dwell on His love with sweetest song,
> And infant voices shall proclaim
> Their early blessings on His name.
> —ISAAC WATTS

7

ABRAHAM: HEADWATERS OF
A MIGHTY STREAM

Genesis 12:1–3, 6–8; 15:1–8; 16:1–16; 17:1–7;
18:9–15; 21:1–13; Hebrews 11:8–16

ONE DAY I STOOD near the mouth of the mighty Amazon where it
empties into the Atlantic Ocean. As I gazed across that vast
expanse of water, I visualized its beginning as a tiny rill,
thousands of miles in the interior of South America. I recalled
that every river has such a beginning, growing in expanse and
volume as it flows along, until somewhere, sometime, it empties
into a seemingly limitless ocean.

Conceived in the heart of God in eternity, the mighty stream
of God's redemptive purpose flows through the ages of history,
finally emptying into eternity with its volume of the saved
multitude which no man can number.

The redemptive purpose was divinely foreseen in Genesis
3:15, and it is evident in God's subsequent dealings with man.
But the historical source of this stream is seen in God's dealings
with Abraham. Other than Jesus Christ, of course, the mountain
peaks in the range of God's dealings with man are Abraham,
Moses, and Paul. Moses took a disordered band of slaves and
constituted them into a covenant nation to be a priest-nation to
the pagan peoples of the earth. Through him, God gave the
law which was to find its fulfillment in Christ. Paul was Christ's
greatest interpreter and evangel. But all this, even the incarna-
tion of God in Christ Jesus, historically stems from Abraham and
God's promise to him.

Genesis 1:1–11:27, while relating true historical events, does not subject itself to the dating processes of historiographers. But with Abraham we are in a historical context as the term is commonly used. Abraham lived about 2000–1900 B.C. Modern archeology has refuted the ideas that he is but a symbol or a folk god idealized as a person. He was a real man, living in a social context not to be identified with the eighth century B.C. but with the time in which Genesis places him. These discoveries have brought him out of the misty folklore of an ancient people into the clear light of historical authenticity. As early as the beginning of this century, S. R. Driver (p. xliv) said that the patriarchal narratives are "substantially accurate" and show "general trustworthiness." Discoveries since that time have removed the words *substantially* and *general*. When we read these narratives, we are at home with the customs and times depicted.

Call and Response

Our exploration of the headwaters of God's mighty stream of redemption begins with Abram's divine *call and his response* to it.

"Now the Lord had said unto Abram, Get thee out of thy country, and from thy kindred, and from thy father's house, unto a land that I will shew thee: And I will make of thee a great nation, and I will bless thee, and make thy name great; and thou shalt be a blessing: And I will bless them that bless thee, and curse him that curseth thee: and in thee shall all families of the earth be blessed" (Gen. 12:1–3).

These three verses are among the most important in the Bible, for they mark the beginning of the outworking in history of God's eternal redemptive purpose. What had been in Jehovah's heart in eternity and had been foreshadowed in Eden (Gen. 3:15) now surfaces in history as God calls one man out of whose line would come him who is the "Lamb slain from the foundation of the world" (Rev. 13:8).

Note that in Genesis 12:1 the Lord "had said." This explains

Genesis 11:31–32. The call came to Abram in Ur of the Chaldees (Acts 7:4), but he spent some time in Haran before going on into Canaan. He probably left Haran about sixty years before his father Terah's death.

Like Paul, Abram could have boasted that he was a citizen of "no mean city," for archeology has shown that Ur was quite a large and important one. Its likely site was what is called today Tel el-Mukayyar, and its principal religion was moon worship. Since Joshua 24:2 says that the ancestors of Israel in Ur "served other gods," there is the strong probability that Terah was a moon worshiper. However, there is growing evidence today that Abram worshiped the true God Jehovah (Davies, p. 118). It is thus understandable why he would respond to a call which meant the complete disruption of his life.

To appreciate what the Lord demanded of Abram we must recognize the importance of country, kindred, and family to the ancients. He was asked to leave all this, perhaps never to return (actually he did not), to strike out for a land unnamed but to which God guided him. It was a venture of sacrificial faith. When one goes to a foreign mission field today, at least he has the prospect of returning home periodically. Abram had no such prospect. Certainly he must have had a deep faith in Jehovah to respond to the call.

However, along with the call there was the promise. Jehovah would make him a great nation, give him a great name, and shower him with blessings, both material and spiritual. The fact that his wife Sarai was barren (Gen. 11:30) makes the promise of a nation all the more a matter of faith. As for the great name, had Abram refused the call, his name would have perished in the dust of the centuries instead of being a household word in the three monotheistic religions of the world (Judaism, Christianity, Islam).

Somewhere I read about two English brothers. One answered the call of God to be a missionary in Africa, and his family sought to dissuade him from burying himself in a pagan land.

The other brother went into government service, declaring that he planned to make a name for himself. Many years later in a British version of "Who's Who," several columns were devoted to the missionary. Under his long list of accomplishments appeared the name of the other brother with the simple words "member of Parliament, brother of ———," the missionary brother. One lost his life only to find it; the other sought to save his life only to lose it.

Abram was also to be a blessing. "In thee shall all families of the earth be blessed." Many competent interpreters translate the verb as a reflexive, "bless themselves." While this is a possible reading, it tones down the meaning—men emulating Abram's example or blessing themselves in his name. The passive form is to be preferred. Charles F. Pfeiffer (p. 42) says, "The Jewish Publication Version (1917) translates the form as passive." Abram is to be the agent through whom Jehovah's blessing will be transmitted to all families of the earth. God's redemptive purpose includes all people. The renewed emphasis upon Abram's being a monotheist shows "that the stature of Abram has no doubt been underestimated in recent biblical scholarship, and perhaps the insights of Genesis and of the New Testament are more likely to be true. . . . After all, Abraham is mentioned between seventy and eighty times in the New Testament" (Davies, p. 169).

Having noted briefly some of the facts in the case, let us now look at the call itself (Gen. 12:1–3). Actually it constitutes a covenant which Jehovah made with Abram, but it was not a conditional covenant such as God made with the nation of Israel (Exod. 19:5–6). At Mount Sinai, three months after Israel's exodus from Egypt, God said, "Now therefore, *if* ye will obey my voice indeed, and keep my covenant, *then* ye shall be a peculiar treasure unto me above all people: for all the earth is mine: And ye shall be unto me a kingdom of priests, and an holy nation" (my italics). As the greater party, Jehovah was not bound by the *then* until Israel fulfilled the *if*. This was a covenant of *law*. History records that Israel did not keep the *if*. So God eventually was not bound by the *then* (see Matt. 21:33–45; 1 Pet. 2:1–10).

In Genesis 12:1–3 no condition is laid down by Jehovah. It was an absolute promise which extended through Abram and his seed to all the families of the earth. It was not a covenant of service as at Sinai; rather it was a covenant of redemption. With no conditions attached to it, it was a covenant of *grace* and pointed to the redemption of all who become spiritual children of Abraham through faith in his seed, Christ (Gal. 3:16). Furthermore, covenants were sealed in blood. Jehovah's covenant to give Canaan to Abram's descendants was sealed in sacrifice (Gen. 15:7–10). The Mosaic covenant was sealed in blood (Exod. 24:1–8), but no such sealing is mentioned in connection with Jehovah's original covenant with Abram. The author of Hebrews says that it was sealed in the blood of Jesus Christ (Heb. 7:22–27; 9:11–26).

The Old Testament often speaks of an everlasting covenant, but this was not the one with Israel at Sinai. The everlasting covenant with David is fulfilled in Christ (2 Sam. 23:5).

Twice the Scriptures speak of the everlasting covenant made with Abraham, Isaac and Jacob (1 Chron. 16:16–18; Psalm 105:6–11) in giving the land of Canaan to them and their seed. Hebrews 13:20 speaks of "the blood of the everlasting covenant" through the death of Christ. This everlasting covenant is, therefore, the redemptive grace covenant made with Abram in Genesis 12:1–3, sealed in the blood of Christ, and pertaining, not to Abram's genetical descendants, but to those who are his descendants through faith (Matt. 3:9; Gal. 3:29).

In response to Jehovah's call, Abram took his wife Sarai and his nephew Lot and went forth. Evidently Lot shared his uncle's faith in Jehovah. One of the briefest phrases on purpose and accomplishment is "and they went forth to go into the land of Canaan; and into the land of Canaan they came" (Gen. 12:5). Since Abram did not know where he was going, why did he take this route? Divine guidance? Yes, but it is true also that he followed the trade route which went toward Egypt. A Semite would more likely follow this route than the one across Asia Minor.

The land of Canaan was occupied by people whose religion was one of the most depraved ever known, centering in sex and child sacrifice. This land, once associated with such unholy things, would one day be called the "Holy Land" because it was to be the center of so much of God's dealings with his people.

Abram entered Canaan and continued southward, passing "through the land unto the place of Sichem" or "Shechem" (RSV). This was in what later was known as Samaria. Here Jehovah told Abram that this was the land to which he had led him, and which he would give to his seed (Gen. 12:7). Abram built there an altar and probably made a sacrifice of thanksgiving. From there he went into the highlands near Bethel, and erected another altar, where he "called upon the name of the Lord" (Gen. 12:8). This evidently means that he claimed the land for Jehovah and his purposes. Basil F. C. Atkinson (p. 119) comments, "In a sea of hideous polytheism the child of God acknowledges the one true and living God." Still journeying southward he came to the "south" or the "Negeb" (RSV). This is the area between Hebron and Beer-sheba. *Negeb* means dryland, describing southern Palestine. So Abram surveyed the land from north to south, going near the border of Egypt.

It is interesting to note the part that altars played in Abram's life—both the building and the absence of them. No mention is made of his erecting an altar in the Negeb. This could be due to the nomadic life he lived there, but when he went into Egypt due to a famine, he built no altar there (Gen. 12:10–20) or later at Gerar (Gen. 20). In both instances, to save his own skin, he palmed off his wife Sarai as his sister. (The fact that she was his half-sister does not alleviate his weak and sinful deed; see 20:12.) The result was that she was taken into the harems of Pharaoh and Abimelech respectively. In both instances, disaster was averted only by an intervention of God. Doubtless these are the lowest points in Abram's life. It is a sad picture to see this man of God being rebuked by pagans! The experience in Egypt probably accounts for Abram's returning to his altar at Bethel (13:3–4). No mention is made of Lot building an altar in Sodom. The remainder of that tragic story is quite familiar (13:5–14:15). After the separation between Lot and Abram, the latter settled in Hebron where he did once again build an altar (13:18).

The incidents of altars and the lack of them suggest that God's people should build *altars* wherever they may reside. Private, family, and public worship will undergird lives, homes, and nations. We neglect to build our altars to our own hurt.

The Bible never glosses over its characters, not even its principal characters. It tells it like it is. For truth is truth, whether it be beautiful or sordid. Despite his human weaknesses Abram was a man of faith, and he followed God by faith where he could not see. Such faith brought him from Ur to Canaan. The historical phase of the drama of redemption had begun.

Faith and Doubt

Abram's case was a mixture of *faith and doubt*. This was especially true with respect to God's promise of the patriarch's seed through which the divine promise was to run. (See Gen. 15–18, 21.)

Abram was seventy-five years old when he entered Canaan. The event recorded in Genesis 15 came probably nine to eleven years after this time. Chapter 14 records his military campaign to rescue Lot from allied invading kings. In keeping with the custom of the time, he returned with the spoils of war, none of which he would keep for himself. It is possible also that he harbored a secret fear that these kings might regroup and come against him with a larger army.

"After these things the word of the Lord came unto Abram in a vision, saying, Fear not, Abram: I am thy shield, and thy exceeding great reward" (15:1). Abram need have no fear of the defeated kings. His reward consisted, not of the spoils of war, but of God himself and that which he held in store for his servant.

The mention of reward stabbed deep into Abram's heart. Events and years had passed since Jehovah's promise of a nation coming out of his loins. He was growing ever older with no evident prospect that the promise would be fulfilled. So he made bold to ask Jehovah for light on the situation. "Lord God, what wilt thou give me, seeing I go childless, and the steward of my house is this Eliezer of Damascus? . . . Behold, to me thou hast given no seed: and, lo, one born in my house is mine heir" (15:2–3).

The Hebrew words translated "Lord God" are *Adonai Elohim.* In Genesis 2–3 this term translates *Jehovah Elohim,* connecting *Elohim,* the creator (Gen. 1), and *Jahweh,* or "Lord Jehovah." *Adonai,* while used of men as lord, when used of Jehovah carries the idea of *helper.* In a sense Abram cried out in his soul, "Jehovah help me!" His longing for an heir was so great, and his faith needed assurance.

As of now his only heir was his steward, a slave in charge of his property. It was the custom for one without an heir to make his steward his heir, but this was a far cry from God's promise.

Jehovah reassured him. "This shall not be thine heir; but he that shall come forth out of thine own bowels shall be thine heir" (15:4). To solidify the promise, the Lord took him out under the night sky and told him to count the stars. So should his seed be. Abram could not count the stars visible to his natural eyes. And how modern telescopes have enlarged this promise! The reference seen in retrospect refers, not to Abram's genetical seed, but to his descendants of faith as seen in the multitude of saints in heaven which no man can number (Rev. 7:9). "So shall thy seed be" (Gen. 15:5).

"And he believed in the Lord; and he counted it to him for righteousness" (15:6). Though Abram's faith had wavered, it now was blown into a burning flame. Not only did he believe Jehovah's word, he believed "in the Lord." The Hebrew reads that he leaned upon him or trusted in him, and his faith was entered into the ledger as *righteousness*. Not that he was righteous without a flaw, but Jehovah regarded him as such, even as he does us when we believe in his Son. Abram and all other Old Testament saints were saved even as we are—through faith in Jehovah—not through knowledge. They did not have the knowledge of God's full redemptive purpose in Christ as do we, but with what knowledge they had, they believed, looking forward to Christ as we look back to his redeeming work. Dimly but surely Abram saw Messiah's day, and was glad (John 8:56).

Paul says that Abram's experience is the norm for all Christian experience (Rom. 4). What was it that the patriarch believed? He believed that God could do what to man is the impossible. "Who against hope believed in hope, that he might become the father of many nations. . . . And being not weak in faith, he considered not his own body now dead, when he was about an hundred years old [when the actual conception took place], neither yet the deadness of Sarah's womb: He staggered not at the promise of God through unbelief; but was strong in faith, giving glory to God; And being fully persuaded that, what he had promised, he was able also to perform. And therefore it was imputed to him for righteousness. Now it was not written for his sake alone, . . . But for us also, to whom it shall be imputed, if we believe on him that raised up Jesus our Lord from the dead; Who was delivered for our offences, and was raised again for our justification" (Rom. 4:18–25).

Like Abram, the lost man must see himself as dead in sin and beyond all human hope. But he must also in full persuasion believe that God can and will keep his promise to save all who believe in him in the person of his Son. Through faith, he who is dead in sin becomes alive in Christ. God declares him righteous as though he had never sinned.

To his covenant of redemption God added the covenant to give Canaan to Abram and his seed. This was sealed in sacrifice

(Gen. 15:7–21). At the same time Jehovah told Abram that before the nation emerging from his loins would do so, they would be in servitude to Egypt. Abram never lived to see this day, but history records its fulfillment.

Why Canaan? Because it was at the heart of the ancient world. Located as a bridge between the continents of Africa, Asia, and Europe, Canaan was the perfect base from which Israel might be a priest-nation to the ancient world. When Israel failed in her covenant, Canaan formed the base from which Christians would operate to preach the gospel of redemption— beginning in Jerusalem and going unto the uttermost part of the earth (Acts 1:8).

This promise also Abram had to accept by faith, for the land was then occupied by the Canaanites. The promise was a long time in being fulfilled, but God's promises are sure. Abram could wait upon the Lord in this instance, but what about the promise of an heir? The advancing ages of both Abram and Sarai made this the pressing need (Gen. 16).

Someone said that Jehovah chose Abram, not because he was so good, but because Jehovah's love was so great. Never do Abram and Sarai appear more like the rest of us than in Genesis 16:1–6. For when the Lord failed to make good his promise immediately, they took matters into their own hands. In the light of Abram's great experience of faith recorded in Genesis 15, we are hardly ready for the event which followed so soon thereafter. But it is often the case that great religious experiences are followed by the letdown of doubt. Thus Satan seeks to counteract our experience of faith.

Despite God's promise, Sarai continued barren. Davies (p. 180) sees the possibility that Abram may have been increasingly difficult to live with because of this delay; so Sarai resorted to an accepted custom of the time. According to archeological records, if a wife were barren, she might give her handmaid to her husband as a secondary wife. Children born in this relationship were considered the children of the real wife. Obviously this was sin against God's ideal of monogamy in marriage.

Nevertheless, Sarai proposed that Abram take her Egyptian slave woman Hagar for this purpose, "and Abram hearkened to the voice of Sarai" (16:2). As Eve led Adam astray, so did Sarai Abram. But when Hagar knew that she was with child, she despised her owner. Sin began to take its toll, as always. When we tamper with the will and ways of God, we always invite tragedy.

Sarai blamed her husband for the outcome, even though it was her idea. Her action reflects the human quality of being unwilling to accept the consequences of our own sins (16:5). And Abram reacted humanly by leaving the solution in his wife's hands. Thus Sarai sent Hagar away. The very custom which was utilized for convenience was violated for the purpose of getting out of an unpleasant situation. According to the Nuzu tablets, if a handmaid bore a child for her mistress, she remained a slave. Should the wife later bear a child, certain rights were set forth for the handmaid and her child. Neither was to be dismissed from the household.

Sent away, Hagar went into the "way of Shur" (16:7). *Shur* means wall. Records of the Twelfth Dynasty of Egypt (circa 2000–1775 B.C.) mention a wall of defense against the Asiatic nomads. The land east of this wall was called the wilderness of Shur. It is natural that Hagar would try to return to her native land, but God had other plans. Here the angel of the Lord appeared, and sent her back to be Sarai's handmaid. This is the first mention in Scripture of "the angel of the Lord." He is usually identified as Jehovah himself in bodily form, hence the second person of the Trinity. He came to Hagar in her time of dire need, even as Christ comes to all men in theirs.

However, the Lord's command was not without a promise. Hagar would bear a son and call him Ishmael ("God hears"). He would be a "wild man" or, literally, "a wild ass of a man," denoting his free, roving character like the wild donkey's. His hand would be against every man, and every man's hand against him. While his descendants would be a great multitude, he would dwell in the midst of his brethren (16:12).

The consequences of the sin of doubt and presumption on the part of Abram and Sarai have been visited, not only upon the third and fourth generation, but even to this present hour. The present-day struggle in the Middle East is a conflict between the descendants of Ishmael and Isaac. God forgives sin, but he does not necessarily remove its temporal results.

Abram was eighty-six years old when Ishmael was born. Thirteen years later, when Abram was ninety-nine years old, Jehovah appeared to him again (Gen. 17). "I am the Almighty God [*El Shaddai*]; walk before me, and be thou perfect. And I will make my covenant between me and thee, and will multiply thee exceedingly" (17:1–2).

Note the name *El Shaddai*. He is the creator God and is powerful to perform his promise concerning Abram's seed. We are reminded of the angel's words to Mary about the virgin birth of Jesus (Luke 1:37), literally, "Because every single word from God shall not be without power." What God says, he can do. Even though Abram's faith had been perplexed by doubt, he is assured that God can and will fulfill his promise.

To reassure his servant God renewed his covenants about Abram's seed and their promised home (Gen. 17:7–8). At this time also Jehovah gave the rite of circumcision as a seal of his promise and extended the promise to include Sarai (17:15–16).

God also changed their names. Abram henceforth shall be called Abraham. *Abram* means "exalted father." *Abraham* means "father of a multitude." Someone has noted that the *h* sound in Hebrew is made by a sharp expulsion of breath. In this light the new name could mean that Jehovah breathed life into a body which Abram considered genetically dead. Shortly thereafter the Lord said that Sarai would henceforth be known as Sarah. *Sarai* is but an old feminine form of *Sarah*, meaning "princess." The changing of names marked a crucial point in their lives. It signaled that the long wait was coming to an end. The time of their parenthood was rapidly approaching. For the first time Abraham's heir's name is given. *Isaac* means "he laughs."

Laughter is mentioned twice in connection with the days before the birth of Isaac. When the Lord told Abraham that Sarah would bear him a son, he fell on his face and laughed. "Shall a child be born unto him that is an hundred years old?" he asked, "and shall Sarah, that is ninety years old, bear" (17:17)? Some see this as a laughter of joy, but the following verse sees it as one of doubt. Despite Jehovah's promise, Abraham said, "O that Ishmael might live before thee!" He still was torn between faith and doubt. Later, when the Lord appeared to Abraham at Mamre, he repeated the promise that Sarah would bear a son (18:10). He even stated the time when he would effect this miraculous conception. "I will surely return to you in the spring, and Sarah your wife shall have a son" (RSV). When Sarah overheard this, she also laughed. That it was doubtful laughter is seen in her denial when the Lord inquired about it (18:12–15). Again the promise is given that nothing is too hard for the Lord; so Isaac's name would ever be a reminder to his parents as to their doubt of God's word.

How marvelous are Jehovah's ways beyond our understanding! No man should ever limit God by his own power or understanding. When faith is tested to the utmost, we should rest in God and leave the unknown to him. It is better to walk with God in the dark than to walk alone in the light. In his own time God will make all things plain.

Nathaniel Hawthorne said, "Christian faith is a grand cathedral, with divinely pictured windows. Standing without you see no glory, nor can imagine any. But standing within every ray of light reveals a harmony of unspeakable splendors." And Augustine said, "Faith is to believe, on the word of God, what we do not see, and its reward is to see and enjoy what we believe."

Fulfillment and Frustration

Abraham and Sarah lived to see the fulfillment of their faith. Yet because of previous doubts, it was an experience of *fulfillment and frustration* (Gen. 21:1–21).

As Jehovah had said, so it happened to Sarah. "For Sarah conceived, and bare Abraham a son in his old age" (21:2). One may wonder why the Lord delayed the event so long, twenty-five years after the first veiled promise was given (12:2). In a sense it was a test of Abraham's faith. Furthermore, when the promise was fulfilled, there must be no question but that it was God's doing alone. While Isaac's birth was not a virgin one, it was miraculous nevertheless. In accord with the Lord's word he was named, and on the eighth day circumcised. What a time of rejoicing it was! This is reflected in Sarah's words, "God hath made me to laugh, so that all that hear will laugh with me" (21:6). The former laughter of incredulity now gave place to the laughter of fulfillment.

Life moved along naturally in Abraham's family, until the time came to wean Isaac. According to custom, this probably took place when he was three to five years old. At this time Ishmael would have been in his middle teen years. To celebrate the occasion the father gave a great feast (21:8). Sarah noted Ishmael "playing with her son Isaac" (21:9, RSV). The King James Version reads "mocking." Interpreters differ as to the sense of this. Paul says that Ishmael "persecuted" Isaac (Gal. 4:29). He likens it to those of the law (son of the bondwoman, Judaizers) persecuting those of grace (son of the free woman). Perhaps the sense is that he played with him in a mocking manner.

At any rate, Sarah resented it, and ordered her husband to send Hagar and her son away. This grieved Abraham, for he also loved Ishmael, but God told him to do it, since "in Isaac shall thy seed be called" (Gen. 21:12). Nevertheless God had concern for Hagar and her son, saving them from dying of thirst in the desert of Paran on the south side of the Negeb. He also promised that Ishmael's descendants would become a great nation (21:13, 18). Henceforth Ishmael dwelt in the desert, becoming an expert archer as were his Bedouin descendants. He married an Egyptian.

The story of Ishmael might have ended there. But almost four thousand years later, the frustration of the conflict between the natural descendants of Ishmael and Isaac still plagues the world.

As Davies notes, Abraham lost his option between the two sons. The seed of promise, as God had said, must run through Isaac alone. This within itself was to cause Abraham great anguish of heart (Gen. 22).

Adventure and Hope

The story is not complete without a brief look at Hebrews 11. In spite of their mingled faith and doubts both Abraham and Sarah merit their places in the Bible's Westminster Abbey of the heroes and heroines of faith. From the vantage point of time, the author of Hebrews says nothing about doubt, but speaks of faith which triumphed in the end. It is a story of *adventure and hope* or assurance.

"By faith" Abraham left Ur to go toward an inheritance, "not knowing whither he went" (Heb. 11:8). His destination was not known. He had no road map. His only guide was his response of faith in God. He went from the known to the unknown. Arriving in the land of promise, he never really possessed it. Rather he became a resident alien (sojourner) in a land held and ruled by pagans. He lived a nomadic life, the only permanence being the pegs of his tent driven in the ground. As a resident alien he paid a tax for the privilege of living and doing business in a land not his own (Heb. 11:9), but by faith he looked up and away from the earthly scene, "for he looked for a city which hath foundations, whose builder and maker is God" (Heb. 11:10). Not a nomad's tent but a city. Not pegs driven into the ground, but a city with permanent foundations. Not a tent pitched each night by his servants, but a city built by God himself.

Likewise, Sarah by faith conceived by one as though he were dead, and out of their union came "so many as the stars of the sky in multitude, and as the sand which is by the sea shore innumerable" (Heb. 11:12). It all began with one seed Isaac, but in reality it was "thy seed, which is Christ" (Gal. 3:16), the seed of faith in him whose day Abraham saw afar off and rejoiced. And the number of that seed, uncountable by man, will not be fully known until all the redeemed of all the ages are gathered in that city which has foundations, whose builder and maker is God. The mighty stream which began with one man of faith flows onward, ever enlarging, until it flows into the unmeasured ocean of eternity.

Abraham, so faithful, yet so frail! Still he stands as a lesson to us all. Walking where he could not see. Stumbling in the dark, but held by the mighty hand of God. And rising to walk again. Not knowing where he went, but still on his way—looking, persevering, waiting; and, in God's own good time, achieving.

In such a path God calls us to walk. Dead in sin, we too are made alive through faith in Christ—Abraham's true seed—and through him we become the true seed of Abraham. Sometimes faltering, failing, and frustrated, but ever held on the course. When our faith becomes as a smoking flax, the omnipotent God fans it again into a flame. By its light we scale the heights as we walk upward to arrive at the city of God.

Resident aliens are we in a strange land. But, like Abraham, we dwell there, doing the business of our King until he says, "Come up higher." And it is all by faith.

> Faith is a grasping of almighty power;
> The hand of man laid on the arm of God;
> The grand and blessed hour
> In which the things impossible to me
> Become the possible, O Lord, through thee.
> —ANONYMOUS

8

ABRAHAM: THE SUPREME TEST OF FAITH

Genesis 22:1–18; Hebrews 11:17–19

> Passive faith but praises in the light,
>   When sun doth shine.
> Active faith will praise in darkest night—
>   Which faith is thine?
> —ANONYMOUS

SOMEONE HAS SAID that "faith is not a sense, nor sight, nor reason, but taking God at his word." That Abraham's was such a faith is evident in the account at hand. His faith in God's promise to give him an heir held on to the trustworthiness of God. Though at times he faltered and stumbled, he lived to see its reward. Jehovah had made it clear that neither Abraham's steward nor Ishmael figured in God's redemptive purpose. It centered in Isaac and none other. For this reason Isaac was all the dearer to him. In him focused, not only a father's natural love, but his faith and hope in the promises of God for the future. For this latter reason the supreme trial of his faith was yet to come.

Demand

Designed to show Abraham's complete acquiescence to Jehovah's will, the *demand* was made at Beer-sheba. "And it came to pass after these things, that God did tempt Abraham, and said unto him, Abraham: and he said, Behold, here I am. And he said,

Take now thy son, thine only son Isaac, whom thou lovest, and get
thee into the land of Moriah; and offer him there for a burnt
offering upon one of the mountains which I will tell thee of"
(Gen. 22:1–2).

"After these things" gathers up the events of Genesis 21. God's
promise of an heir had been honored. Ishmael had been sent
away, leaving the patriarch with Isaac alone. A resolving of a
difference had been made with Abimelech, and Abraham settled at Beer-sheba to live in peace. With a sense of triumphant
faith he looked to the future. The struggle was over; now life
could move along its cool sequestered way. Then came the supreme test of Abraham's life. For the Lord made one final, painful demand of his faith. It involved, not only a father's love for his
son, but also his faith in God's promise. as to his seed.

In the Hebrew text *God* is in the emphatic position; so the
author clearly shows that the test was initiated by God himself.
The word *tempt* may mean that, but it basically means to test.
Satan tests us to prove us evil—that is, he tempts. God tests us
to prove us genuine. This is the sense of the word here.

In whatever way God communicated with Abraham, perhaps
in a dream, he made the supreme demand of him. "Take now thy
son, thine only son, whom thou lovest." Isaac was not only the
son of promise but the object of his father's love. Abraham was
told to take him into the land of Moriah to a place that God
would show him. Again the patriarch was called to *go out,* not
knowing where he went. This time it meant not merely leaving
his native land and family, but giving up his only beloved son
as a burnt offering. A burnt offering was completely consumed
by fire on an altar. To Abraham it signified the absolute physical
loss of him in whom God's redemptive promise was to run and
therefore seemed such an unreasonable demand.

As we look into Abraham's heart and mind, we may see both
poignant pain and mental perplexity. The son for whom he had
waited so long—was it to end like this? Had God really told him
to do this? Or had he merely imagined it? Was it a revelatory

dream or just a nightmare? To see Abraham otherwise is to make him a dry stick and not a man.

The things which perplexed Abraham have bothered many interpreters of the event. Some see the event as a parable—God's repudiating pagan child sacrifice. Others compare Isaac to Israel —called into being, rejected, and then brought to life again. Others say it is a story of Abraham's obedience. However, the context gives no real evidence of a parable. That God repudiated child sacrifice is not to be questioned. The story hardly fits Israel since it centers, not in Isaac, but in Abraham. Furthermore, the complete biblical story of the nation Israel ends in rejection, not in complete restoration (see Matt. 21:33–45). Certainly, the story depicts the obedience of the patriarch.

Some interpreters say that Abraham mistakenly *thought* that God told him to sacrifice Isaac. This is based upon our concept of God as love and the event as a violation of the Christian conscience. However, the event should be seen in its own context, not transported into the realm of Christian hindsight. It fits perfectly into its own time. Furthermore, while God's love permeates all other of his attributes, it should not be limited to itself alone or considered in absolute isolation.

I see Abraham's experience exactly as the Scripture relates it. It was a real experience in which God did test Abraham's faith by telling him to sacrifice his son Isaac. Of course, God knew from the beginning what he would do, but if this was to be a genuine test, he could not reveal the outcome to his servant.

The event is related to the time and religious environment in which Abraham lived. The Canaanites practiced child sacrifice in their worship of the fire god Molech. So the test could be seen as God asking the patriarch if he loved Jehovah as much as these pagans loved their god. It is true that Jehovah did not approve of this heathen practice (Lev. 18:21; 20:2–3), but at this point in God's revelation Abraham did not know this. Surely he must have reasoned about the matter. Even beyond the pagan aspects of this cruel practice, he wrestled with a father's love. Beyond this, however, was the promise of his seed through Isaac. Still, he had Jehovah's clear commandment. Though blundering at times, he had met the test of faith that despite natural difficulties the Lord would give him an heir. Was he now to be destroyed? If so, what of the promise? What of God's redemptive purpose? Surely in this event Abraham faced the supreme test of his faith.

Every act of faith is acting beyond one's knowledge. If we go only as far as we can see, we walk not by faith but by sight. If I could understand God, 1 could not worship him. It would mean that my mind is greater than his, that I am superior to him. This is why I must live by faith in him—trusting where I cannot understand; walking where I cannot see; knowing that I do not walk alone—for he walks before me. He does not ask me to do what he has not already done.

We cannot fail to see the parallel between God's demand upon Abraham and what he himself had already done, for he too has an "only son, whom [he] lovest." Even though the historical enactment of making his Son a *burnt offering* for man's sin was centuries in the future, already in eternity he had given him to be slain for man's redemption (Rev. 13:8). Could man have been redeemed by gold and silver, God could have given mountains of it and have had plenty left. Even heavenly bodies he has without number. But no such could suffice for our sin. "The wages of sin is death" (Rom. 6:23). Not just any death, but the death of the Son of God alone could suffice to pay that debt. The plan called for God to give all that he had. He has only one Son; so he surrendered to man's need in giving his all and best. This is what God asked of Abraham—not a part of his flocks and herds, but *all he had,* his only son "Isaac, whom thou lovest."

There was no argument or delay with God's will. Early the next morning Abraham made the necessary preparations, including wood for the fire and a container with fire (Gen. 22:6). He took two servants—and Isaac—and departed (22:3). Evidently he said nothing to Sarah, for this was a decision which he alone could make, with no outside interference.

On the third day he sighted the place where the sacrifice was to take place (22:4). It was in the "land of Moriah." The Septuagint reads "lofty" rather than "Moriah." The Syriac reads "land of the Amorites." The Samaritan suggestion that the original reading was "Oak of Moreh" (Shechem) is ruled out because of the distance and travel time from Beer-sheba. Mount Moriah in Jerusalem, where Solomon later built the Temple (2 Chron. 3:1) fits the conditions of the narrative. Where later the blood of animal sacrifice would flow, insofar as Abraham could see, the blood of his son would be shed.

Deliverance

The pathos of the following scene is almost impossible for us to grasp. Yet it ended in *deliverance*. Leaving the two servants at the foot of the mountain, Abraham said, "I and the lad will go yonder and worship, and come again unto you" (Gen. 22:5). How may we understand "I and the lad . . . will come again unto you"? Abraham knew that he would slay the lad and that his body would be consumed by fire, yet somehow both father and son would later descend the mountain they were about to ascend. Abraham's statement can be explained only by an undaunted faith. In man's view the sacrifice was to close his eyes to the past and shut the door to the future—but still the patriarch held on to his faith.

The author of Hebrews interprets it for us. "By faith Abraham, when he was tried, offered up Isaac: and he that had received the promises offered up his only begotten son, Of whom it was said, That in Isaac shall thy seed be called: Accounting that God was able to raise him up, even from the dead; from whence also he received him in a figure" (Heb. 11:17–19). Abraham did not understand God's demand. Had he done so he would have acted out of other than faith. But his faith in God's promise was so firmly fixed that he reasoned that, despite the present circumstance, God would still work out his purpose—even if it meant raising Isaac from the dead. He firmly expected that both he and Isaac would descend the mountain together. However, this was an expectation based upon faith, not upon knowledge, and it does not alleviate the demand made upon Abraham; neither did it ease the pain in his heart.

In the light of the obvious parallel between this event and the death of God's Son, I cannot ignore Jesus' promise to his disciples that after the dying, "I will come to you" (John 14:18). This he did, not only after the resurrection, but in the presence of the Holy Spirit (John 14:16–18).

Abraham placed the wood for the burnt offering on Isaac. Jesus also bore the wood of his sacrifice to Calvary. Abraham himself took the consuming fire and a knife in his hand. Is it stretching the suggestion too far in seeing that God's fire (wrath against sin poured out on his Son) was held in his hand, along with the knife (God's giving of his Son's life)? Notice that "they went up both of them together" (Gen. 22:6). Whatever was the will of his father, Isaac was one in it.

Obviously one thing was missing, and Isaac asked, "Where is the lamb for a burnt offering?" (22:7). Was this question asked out of a child's curiosity, or was the grim reality of the occasion beginning to dawn upon him? Perhaps he had noted the painful ordeal reflected in his father's face, hardly one to be experienced in anticipated worship. Was he himself to be the sacrifice? Isaac must have been familiar with the practice among the Canaanites.

Abraham's reply must have served only to deepen this growing impression in Isaac's mind. "My son, God will provide himself a lamb for a burnt offering" (22:8). There were no flocks about. Whence would come this lamb? A lamb was a young sheep; he as a child was a *young man*. Was he to be the *lamb* after all? "So they went both of them together" (22:8).

The repetition of this statement from verse 6 is important. In the former it could be a matter-of-fact statement, but the latter suggests more. Isaac trusted his father's word about the lamb. If he suspected that he was the lamb, he did not flee down the mountain in terror. Rather "they went both of them together." So be it, whatever the end might be. What was done would be a blending of their wills with God's will. It suggests Jesus' words in Gethsemane. If there is no other way—"not as I will, but as thou wilt" (Matt. 26:39). These words summarize the actions of both Abraham and Isaac.

God asks for our best—our all—and it is the very essence of faith to give it. Our minds may ask *why?* But without an answer, through faith our wills submit. In his own time God makes all things plain. But in the meantime, we must follow on to know the Lord.

Arriving at the place of sacrifice, Abraham built an altar out of stones. He laid the wood on it in order. Then he bound his son and laid him upon the wood. At this point there could be no doubt whatever in Isaac's mind as to his being the *lamb,* but no cry of protest is heard from him. Atkinson (p. 199) says, "In this he showed himself a true pattern of his great Descendant. Perhaps in the feelings of Isaac at this moment we may trace a faint shadow of the terrible dereliction of the Saviour, when He was cut off from the presence of the Father, endured His curse, and suffered perdition in our stead (Matt. 27:46; Gal. 3:13)."

However, the center of the story is Abraham, not Isaac. There is no more dramatic scene in all the Bible or in any other literature. "And Abraham stretched forth his hand, and took the knife to slay his son" (Gen. 22:10). A thousand times he would gladly have exchanged places with Isaac, but this was not God's command. He was to sacrifice his son, not himself. He had to give God his best, and his best was not his aged body or life soon to end. Not his second-best, but his best! And that *best* was his son, yea, the son of promise. Again the parallel—for God "spared not his own Son" (Rom. 8:32). Rather he was in Christ, reconciling the world unto himself (2 Cor. 5:19). God's redemptive purpose could run only through those who compared finitely with the infinite Father and Son. Such he found in Abraham and Isaac.

When Abraham lifted the knife, poised and ready to plunge it into the heart of his son, he had already in his will given Isaac completely to God. There remained but the downward plunge of the lethal blade, but in the father's will he was already dead. Francisco (p. 32) says, "The writer is saying that not until Abraham acted upon his faith did that faith come to fruition. Until he lifted the knife over his son, the ultimate surrender to God had not occurred. Faith is not just a nice attitude toward God; it is submission to his will. To will is not enough. The act is the ultimate test." The overt act, whether good or bad, is but an expression of the surrender of the will.

At this climactic split-second, Jehovah stayed Abraham's hand. "And the angel of the Lord called unto him out of heaven, and said, Abraham, Abraham: and he said, Here am I" (Gen. 22:11). The repetition of Abraham's name suggests the urgency and triumph of the moment. Had the patriarch not heard or heeded the voice, the knife already would have been plunged into Isaac's heart. But he had stood the test, and the Lord stopped him. Previously in this chapter the name *God* has been used, but here the writer uses *Lord* or *Jehovah,* God's redeeming name. He redeemed Isaac's life from destruction.

Therefore, Jehovah said, "Lay not thine hand upon the lad, neither do thou any thing unto him: for now I know that thou fearest [reverence] God, seeing thou hast not withheld thy son, thine only son from me" (22:12). At that very moment Abraham saw a ram caught in a thicket by its horns (22:13). God had provided the sacrifice after all, and for Abraham it was a sacrifice of thanksgiving indeed!

The story would not be complete if we did not note that what God did for Abraham, he did not do for himself. He provided no substitute for his Son whom he loves. He went all the way as his

Son paid the price for the sin of the world and became the divine substitute for all who will receive him as Savior.

Divine Assurance

Because Abraham had been proved faithful to the uttermost, Jehovah renewed his previous promises. He gave him *divine assurance* that the promises would stand. Actually, Jehovah took an oath by himself, since there is no greater by whom to swear. The angel of the Lord is the preincarnate Christ.

"By myself have I sworn, saith the Lord, for because thou hast done this thing, and hast not withheld thy son, thine only son: That in blessing I will bless thee, and in multiplying I will multiply thy seed as the stars of the heaven, and as the sand which is upon the sea shore; and thy seed shall possess the gate of his enemies; And in thy seed shall all the nations of the earth be blessed; because thou hast obeyed my voice" (Gen. 22:16–18).

Interpreters note that Jehovah made fourteen promises to Abraham. These verses are the final promises and repeat some of the previous promises, but one new one is added: "Thy seed shall possess the gate of his enemies." This is a promise of victory. History records that Abraham's natural descendants often suffered military defeat, but this promise evidently involved his "seed, which is Christ" (Gal. 3:16). His enemies shall be made the footstool of his feet (Ps. 110:1; 1 Cor. 15:25; Heb. 10:12–13). The last enemy to be destroyed is death (1 Cor. 15:26). This is a promise fulfilled in the victorious lives of Christians, the spiritual seed of Abraham.

It should be noted, however, that the last of these promises repeats the one made in Genesis 12:3: "In thy seed shall all the nations of the earth be blessed." God's redemptive purpose includes all men, not Jews alone; there is no room for narrow prejudice—whatever its base. All nations, all people are the objects of his love which has gone out and down the ages. It flows from the heart of God, to be sure, but historically it stems from one who was mighty in faith, one to whom God affirmed his promises "because thou hast obeyed my voice" (Gen. 22:18). It rushes on today as a mighty stream through Abraham's "seed, which is Christ," who gave his life for the sin of the world. God has provided the sacrifice, that all who believe in him may have everlasting life.

For all practical purposes the story of Abraham ends here, and it is a fitting end. He returned to Beer-sheba, later moved to Hebron, buried Sarah there, and later provided a wife for Isaac. Abraham married a second time (25:1). His second wife was Keturah, and she bore him six sons. Finally, at the age of one hundred and seventy-five years Abraham died and was buried alongside Sarah. To this day you may see what is reported to be their tomb in a mosque in Hebron. One might well place above his tomb the epitaph "Faithful to the Uttermost."

Abraham stands as a finite commentary upon Paul's words declaring God's infinite love. "God was in Christ, reconciling the world unto himself."

Many years ago I preached in a revival in Birmingham, Alabama, at the Powderly Baptist Church where Henry L. Lyon, Jr., my brother-in-love (not "law"), was pastor. During this time we sought to win a man to faith in Christ, but like many before us, we were unsuccessful. Some months later I became the pastor of another church in that city. One morning Dr. Lyon called me to go with him to see this man in the hospital—at the man's request. There we heard the following story:

"I have received Christ as my Savior. It happened like this. My little son and I were walking along the street. Suddenly he ran into the street in front of a large truck which was bearing down upon him. I knew that if it hit him he would most likely be killed. In a split second I realized that I did not have time to catch him and bring him back to safety. So I plunged into the street, knocking him beyond the truck's path but leaving my own body there. As I did so, I knew that I probably would die in the act.

"When I came to, here in the hospital, I realized for the first time how God in Christ could so love me that he would die to save me. And I trusted him as my Savior. The first Sunday I am able I will be at the church service to make this confession publicly." And this he did.

Faintly down the centuries comes this truth from the story of Abraham, but at Calvary it burst into a crescendo, as God gave his *only Son whom he loves* to die for our sins. "For God so loved the world, that he gave his only begotten son, that whosoever believeth in him should not perish, but have everlasting life" (John 3:16).

9

JACOB: A STUDY IN SHADOW AND LIGHT

Genesis 25:20–34; 27:1–35:29

DESPITE THE GREAT EMPHASIS upon the long-awaited birth of Isaac, the Scriptures record comparatively little about him as a man. He is little more than a bridge between Abraham and Jacob. The Bible does not give complete biographies of its characters; it records primarily the development of God's redemptive purpose. Since it was out of Jacob that the twelve tribes of Israel, God's covenant nation, would come, the greater emphasis is upon him.

As a man, Isaac appears to have been a somewhat weak character. This probably reflects the overly protected life that he lived. Since he was Abraham's son of promise, he seems to have been sheltered by his doting father. For example, Isaac was not permitted to leave the land of promise in search for a wife among his father's own people. Rather his father sent his steward to select one for him (Gen. 24). At any rate the narrative largely passes by Isaac to hasten on to the life of Jacob, his son.

Cunning

Jacob's life was indeed one of "shadow and light." That he was a *cunning* man is evident in the story of his birth. When Isaac was forty years old, he married Rebekah, but she was childless for twenty years. This is a familiar story (see Rachel, Gen. 29:31; Hannah, 1 Sam. 1:2; Elizabeth, Luke 1:7). It seems apparent that in each of these cases God's purpose was to demonstrate clearly his peculiar presence and power.

Finally, in answer to Isaac's prayer, Rebekah conceived, and gave birth to twin boys. During her pregnancy she experienced great difficulty as the boys struggled in her womb—a harbinger of things to come. When she inquired of the Lord as to her condition, she was told that "two nations are in thy womb, and two manner of people shall be separated from thy bowels: and the one people shall be stronger than the other people; and the elder shall serve the younger" (Gen. 25:23).

The separation does not refer to the birth itself. "And two peoples, born of you, shall be divided" (RSV). So the division was to be between the boys after birth. This is ultimately seen in the future of the two nations, Israel and Edom. It was, however, evident in the twin boys themselves.

Esau, "red" and "hairy," was the first to be born. *Esau* means to press or squeeze, but in Hebrew *red* is *Edom. Seir,* a synonym for Esau, means "hairy." So both his name and destiny are described in his condition at birth. When the second son was born, it was found that he had taken hold of his brother's heel (RSV) as though even then he sought to be the firstborn. Hence he was called *Jacob.* The Hebrew word for "heel" is *akob.* Prefixed by the small letter in the Hebrew alphabet, it comes out as *Jacob,* which means "may God protect." But when the shortened form, minus the name for God, is used, it is interpreted in terms of "heel" or "he takes by the heel" "the supplanter." Francisco (p. 40) calls him "the heel snatcher." In the light of future events, however we interpret the incident at his birth, *Jacob* is known as the supplanter, trickster, or beguiler.

This difference in the twin brothers is clearly brought out in Genesis 25:27–34. Esau became a "skilful hunter" (RSV). He wandered here and there in search for food and took it where he found it. Jacob, on the other hand, was a shepherd, living a quiet, well-ordered life. This is the meaning of "a plain man" (25:27). The seed for forthcoming trouble also lay in the fact that the parents played favorites. Isaac loved Esau, and Rebekah loved Jacob. This is probably due to the fact that each parent saw in his/her favorite son the qualities which were opposite to theirs: the quiet Isaac wished he were like Esau; the restless Rebekah found fulfillment in the well-ordered life of Jacob. When parents have pets among their children, they are asking for trouble.

One day Esau came in famished from the hunt. Jacob had made some lentil soup. When Esau asked for some of the soup, Jacob acted true to his nature. "Sell me this day thy birthright" (25:31). His brother was such a slave to his fleshly appetite that he agreed, saying that if he did not eat he would die. What good would his birthright do him then? Tantalizing his brother with the food, Jacob made him swear that he would sell him his birthright. And Esau did. He filled his stomach and went his way, little realizing what he had done. "Thus Esau despised his birthright" (25:34).

It is most likely that Jacob's mother had told him of the words of God to her prior to his birth (25:23). This does not excuse Jacob's behavior. On the other hand, it reveals Esau's nature and how cheaply he regarded the birthright. His physical appetite came first. Jacob, like a shrewd businessman, paid only what the owner placed as the value on the item in the transaction.

What did the birthright involve? According to custom the firstborn was to receive two-thirds of his father's estate, the younger getting only one-third. Furthermore, the older became the head of the family at the father's death. This involved not only family authority but also spiritual responsibility. In the case at hand this involved the promise of God with respect to his redemptive purpose.

Obviously God could hardly use such a man as Esau in this. Malachi 1:2–3 says, "I loved Jacob, and I hated Esau" (see also Rom. 9:13). This does not refer to emotion but to choice. Even though Esau was the firstborn, in his sovereign will God could not trust the redemptive promises to a man of his nature; so he chose Jacob. Granted, at the outset Jacob was far from being the man God could use, but he possessed the qualities which could be transformed and molded into an instrument of spiritual service. Is not this true with all of us? God uses imperfect people since they are all that he has, but by his redeeming and enabling grace he molds and makes us after his will. Surely everyone who serves Christ must say with Paul, "By the grace of God I am what I am" (1 Cor. 15:10).

What Jacob began by his cunning, his mother completed by trickery (Gen. 27), and Jacob was a willing, if fearful, partner in it all.

"Isaac was old, and his eyes were dim, so that he could not see" (27:1). He did not know when he would die but feared that the time might be near. (Actually he lived many years; see 35:28.) He determined to bestow his blessing which was considered as a last will and testament. Once bestowed, even orally, it could not be changed. This fact is borne out by the Nuzu tablets.

Whether or not Isaac was aware of Esau's foolish bargain in selling his birthright is not stated. Probably he was. But since the blessing normally went to the elder son, he called Esau to him. His favorite son was told to kill a deer and prepare its meat as he liked it. Having eaten it, he would bestow his blessing upon him. In so doing he would disregard both God's word and Esau's bargain.

Evidently Rebekah overheard the conversation. She certainly knew of her pet son's bargain with Esau; so she set in motion a scheme to nail down the bargain for Jacob. That God had told her that Jacob would eventually rule over Esau does not alleviate her guilt. Both a schemer and a grabber, Rebekah was not one to sit and wait upon the Lord. Someone asked a man if his wife had a will of her own. He replied, "I'll say she does. She even writes her diary a month in advance." She wrote it, and then made it happen. Rebekah was such a woman.

If Jacob inherited his father's quiet nature, he also inherited his mother's cunning. As soon as Esau left on his hunt, Rebekah went to work. She told Jacob to bring two kids from the goats. These she would prepare to Isaac's liking, and Jacob, carrying the dish to his father, pretending to be Esau, would trick his father into giving him the blessing. Rebekah was not so much concerned about Isaac's death as she was about the future of her *pet* (27:9). It is not a pretty picture, but the Bible tells it as it is.

Jacob was hesitant to proceed with the scheme, not out of ethics, but out of fear (27:11–17). Since his brother was a hairy man, should his father feel Jacob's smooth skin he would discover the ruse. Then rather than bless him, he would curse him. But Rebekah assumed to herself any dire consequences. To perpetrate the fraud she dressed Jacob in Esau's clothes and put goat skins on his hands and about his neck. Then the evil plan was set in motion.

Jacob went to his father, identifying himself as Esau. When Isaac asked how he had come so quickly, he said that God had enabled him to make a quick kill. Thus he added a second lie to the first, even involving God in it (27:18–20). Evidently the old man suspected trickery and asked to feel his son. When his hands touched the goat's hair, he said, "The voice is Jacob's voice, but the hands are the hands of Esau" (27:22). This statement has become synonymous with deceit. Still not satisfied, Isaac asked, "Art thou my very son Esau? And he said, I am" (27:24). Another lie! After he had eaten, Isaac tried one final test. He kissed his son and in so doing smelled the clothes Jacob was wearing—probably dirty and sweaty. This convinced him that it was Esau, so he gave him the blessing (27:28–29).

Note that this blessing contained no spiritual content. "The dew of heaven" referred to moisture which would give the ground a good yield. The blessing furthermore included lordship over people, nations, and his family. It also included curse and blessing respectively upon those who did either to his son.

Thus did Jacob and his mother steal the birthright. Had they but waited upon the Lord! As with Ishmael and Isaac, they set in motion forces of enmity between the descendants of Jacob and Esau which continue to this day.

> O what a tangled web we weave,
> When first we practice to deceive!
> —Sir Walter Scott

Hardly had Jacob departed with the blessing, when Esau returned (27:30–40). When the perfidy was revealed, it was too late. The oral blessing could not be recalled. Instead, at Esau's insistence, with bitter tears, Isaac gave him a secondary blessing. Centuries later the author of Hebrews warned his readers against being sensuous people "as Esau, who for one morsel of meat sold his birthright. For ye know how that afterward, when he would have inherited the blessing, he was rejected: for he found no place of repentance, though he sought it carefully with tears" (Heb. 12:16–17). Opportunity despised is opportunity lost. While God certainly did not approve of the deceit of Rebekah and Jacob, he overruled the evil to accomplish his benevolent, righteous purpose.

However, this clever cunning was not the end. For "Esau hated Jacob . . . and Esau said in his heart, The days of mourning for my father are at hand; then will I slay my brother Jacob" (Gen. 27:41). This is the dire end of parental favoritism and a divided family.

Hearing of Esau's resolve, Rebekah enlisted Isaac's aid to send Jacob away. He was to go to her brother Laban at Haran to seek a wife from among her people. This purpose in itself was noteworthy, but the occasion was sad indeed. Rebekah did not expect Jacob to be away long, but she hoped that Esau would change his attitude in the meantime (27:43–45). As it was, Jacob was gone for more than twenty years, during which time his mother apparently died. Insofar as the record shows, she never saw him again. The curse of the whole thing did indeed fall on her (27:13). The record suggests that Esau also left home after

Jacob's departure. So the plotting mother, in effect, lost both her sons.

One cannot play fast and loose with God's righteous will. Trickery may gain a point here and there, but it loses in the end. Even if we escape for the moment, each of us has a rendezvous with God at the final judgment. "Be not deceived; God is not mocked [you cannot turn up your nose at God and get away with it]: for whatsoever a man soweth, that shall he also reap" (Gal. 6:7). This is true whether we sow bad or good (Gal. 6:8). Indeed, the law of nature teaches that we reap more than we sow —the same quality, but greater in quantity!

Jacob's experience left him subdued, but his cunning nature remained. This is evident in the familiar scene at Bethel (Gen. 28:10–22). The supplanter or trickster recognized in the ladder to heaven that he had had a confrontation with God. (We may flee the scene of our sins, but we cannot flee from God's presence.) So he called the place, formerly called Luz, *Bethel,* the house of God (Hebrew: *Beth,* house; *El,* God).

At this point Jacob's nature took over, and he sought to strike a bargain with God. Once he had told his brother that if he would give him his birthright, he would give him his soup. Now to God himself he says, "If God will be with me, and will keep me in this way that I go, and will give me bread to eat, and raiment to put on, So that I come again to my father's house in peace [save him from Esau]; then shall the Lord be my God: And this stone, which I have set for a pillar, shall be God's house: and of all that thou shalt give me I will surely give the tenth unto thee" (Gen. 28:20–22).

If it were not so tragic, it would be funny. In covenants the greater party sets the conditions. (Note *if* and *then* in Exod. 19:5–6.) But here the lesser party sets the terms: *If* God will do certain things, *then* Jacob will acknowledge him as his God.

Before condemning Jacob, we should look to ourselves. If God will bless and protect us, our families and our business, then we will worship and serve him. Such is not faith before the fact, but fact before faith. It requires no faith at all to practice such a religion. When things go well, we take the credit. When they go wrong, we blame God. God will be no party to such a "Heads I win, tails God loses" religion.

How many people practice the tithe with the spirit of Jacob! If God gives you a dollar, you will give him a dime. Any pagan would agree to such an arrangement! God is under no obligation to bless such materially or spiritually. We must trust him with all we are and have—and trust the God of all the earth to do right. The fact that God later did bless Jacob is not due to his bargain but to God's sovereign grace and to the fulfillment of his redemptive purpose.

Finally Jacob arrived at Haran. When he met Rachel, it was love at first sight (Gen. 29:1–18). The highest moment in Jacob's life up to this point was his love for Rachel, but he was still the cunning trickster. However, in Laban, his mother's brother, he almost met his match. Such cunning seems to have run in the family.

About a month after Jacob's arrival at his uncle's dwelling, Laban brought up the matter of wages (29:15). Evidently Jacob had made himself useful. He was ambitious but not lazy. The writer notes that Laban had two daughters. The elder was Leah; the younger, Rachel. Leah was "tender eyed." Interpreters differ as to the meaning of this. Some see her as having weak eyes, but probably they were dull, lacking the luster which Easterners associated with beauty. Rachel, on the other hand, was beautiful (29:17). Since Jacob loved Rachel, he offered to work for Laban seven years if he might marry her. Apparently he had no dowry to offer her father (32:10). It was agreed.

But after the seven years, Laban passed Leah off on Jacob by a trick (29:21–25). How this was done is not stated. Davies (p. 222) suggests that Jacob must have been very drunk from the wedding feast. The bridal feast was literally a drinking feast (29:22). At any rate, the next morning when Jacob discovered the trick, he faced Laban with it. The father fell back on the custom that the older daughter must marry before the younger one (29:26). The irony is that whereas Jacob, the younger, had supplanted his older brother, he now found that the older sister had supplanted the younger as his bride. His chickens had come home to roost!

Let it be noted in his favor that Jacob took it like a good sport. If he could dish it out, he could also take it. He completed the week of marriage feast for Leah with the understanding that he might then marry Rachel also (29:27–28). But he promised to work another seven years for her.

Genesis 29:31–30:24 records the birth of eleven of Jacob's sons. In all Leah bore him six sons and one daughter; her handmaid bore him two. But Rachel was barren. To provide him with *her* sons she resorted to the custom of letting her handmaid bear them, who bore him two sons. Finally, Rachel bore him a son whom she named Joseph, saying that the Lord would give her another son (30:24). All of Jacob's sons except Benjamin were born in Haran. These sons became *tribes,* comprising the covenant priest-nation through which Jehovah proposed to spread his redemptive purpose. The rill which began in Abraham is beginning to widen into a stream, gathering volume and momentum as it wends its way in history.

After Joseph's birth, Jacob decided to return to Canaan (30:25–26). During his stay at Haran, Laban had prospered. He recognized this as the Lord's blessing because of Jacob, so he sought to persuade Jacob to stay, with an offer of increased wages. Here began another *deal* proposed by the cunning Jacob. Refusing wages, he asked that he be given all of the flocks and herds which were not pure white. Laban, figuring this would be a comparatively small number, agreed, but by a clever ruse Jacob saw to it that the opposite was true (30:37–43).

Finally, Jacob determined to get away, prompted by a word from Jehovah (31:11–13). While Laban was away shearing his sheep, Jacob gathered his family and property to return to Canaan. Figuring that their father had not been fair with them and Jacob, Leah and Rachel agreed to go, but before leaving Rachel stole her father's household gods (31:19).

They slipped away during Laban's absence. When he learned of Jacob's departure, Laban pursued him, overtaking him at Mount Gilead, an area north of the river Jabbok just south of the Sea of Galilee and east of the Jordan River. The Lord had told Laban to speak neither good nor evil to Jacob; so he complained that Jacob had left so secretly, without a feast or allowing Laban to kiss his daughters before they left. Jacob said his manner of departure was to prevent Laban from refusing to let his daughters go with him (31:25–31).

Also Laban accused Jacob of stealing his household gods (31:30). These gods or *teraphim* were important to Laban. According to the Nuzu tablets, the one possessing them could claim a legal right to the family estate, which explains why Rachel had taken them. She did not want her father to defraud her husband. Jacob knew nothing of his wife's action. He was so certain that the gods were not in his group, he gave Laban permission to search every tent. If they were found the one taking them should die. The Code of Hammurabi provided this penalty for anyone stealing the property of a god or temple.

The search of other tents failed to reveal the gods. When Laban came to Rachel's tent, she was sitting upon "the camel's furniture" (saddle?) in which she had hidden the gods. Shrewdly she asked not to be made to stand up, since "the custom of women" (monthly period) was upon her (31:35). A search of the rest of the tent proved fruitless.

Angered at Laban's charge, Jacob took full advantage of the situation. "All of the frustration and resentment of twenty years' toil came welling up" (Francisco, p. 39). Finally, they reached an agreement to part in peace. A stone was set up as a witness to this. It was called "Mizpah." "The Lord watch between me and thee, when we are absent one from another" (31:49). This has come to be a beautiful prayer of parting. However, its original meaning was quite different. It contains elements of mistrust.

Actually Jacob said that the Lord should keep an eye on Laban when he could not see what he was doing. Mutually it was agreed that the Lord should serve as a lookout to prevent either from planning evil against the other. Out of past experiences neither trusted the other.

Divisions, whether in family or larger groups, wound the heart of God. In Christ he has broken down the middle wall of partition (Eph. 2:14). His purpose is to make of two one new man, so making peace (Eph. 2:15). God's ideal will become a reality only when his reign is established in men's hearts. We are still far from the reality. But we are to continue striving to this end through the proclamation of the gospel of reconciliation of man to God and men to men.

Change

Up to this point Jacob hardly seems like a man whom God could use, but in his own time and way God used even Jacob's misdeeds to effect a *change* in him. It cannot be repeated too often that while God does not will men's evil deeds, he works within their context to effect repentance and transformation. Some of his most effective servants have been those, once steeped in sin, who were saved from it and to God's purpose. This does not justify sin, but it shows what God's grace can do for and to one who submits to it.

Following his meeting with Laban, Jacob and his company continued their journey southward. Jacob knew that every step brought him nearer to a showdown with Esau. His cunning nature still is in control as evidenced by his preparation for this meeting (Gen. 32:3 ff.). He sent messengers to inform his brother that he was coming. In his message he mentioned his riches, probably to suggest that a peaceful welcome by Esau might be to his brother's advantage. Note that he called Esau "my lord" (32:5), possibly to remove the sting of his possession of the birthright.

The messengers returned with alarming news. Esau was on his way with four hundred men. To Jacob this could only mean hostilities, so he set about to prepare for the worst. He divided his company into two camps, hoping that should his brother destroy one, the other might escape. And then he prayed (32: 9–12).

This is the first recorded prayer of Jacob. As one has noted, previously there had been much religious talk, but no prayer. Jacob had lived by his wits, accepting God's grace but giving nothing in return. Now he faced a situation with which he alone could not cope. Many a person has been driven to prayer and to God by desperation, but Jacob's prayer was a good one. He addresses Deity as both the *God* of his fathers and *Jehovah* (Lord) who told him to return to Canaan. Jacob first acknowledged God's blessings (32:9). Then he confessed his unworthiness (32:10). Next he prayed for deliverance from Esau. He showed concern for his family (32:11). Finally, he reminded God of his promise (32:12).

But still he was the cunning Jacob. For he arranged three bands of animals to be sent at intervals as presents to Esau. Hopefully by the time Esau reached him these gifts would have assuaged his wrath. That night he sent his family and goods over the Jabbok. But he remained behind. "Jacob was left alone" (32:24). Barnhouse (vol. 2, p. 121) says, "Jacob had schemed and prayed, and planned and prayed, and connived and prayed, and now he was spent and alone." One may well imagine his anxious heart—alone in the dark. But more—he was alone with God.

Genesis 32:24 introduces the supreme crisis in Jacob's life. He was awaiting the dramatic meeting with Esau, but the great crisis was with himself. It was a spiritual crisis. We may well believe that all which had happened to Jacob led him to see himself as he was, so he had sought solitude in order to do some soul-searching. If he expected to meet God, it took place in an unexpected manner.

Suddenly out of the darkness there sprang a man who seized Jacob. Perhaps he thought that it was his brother, so to Jacob he was fighting for his life—in the darkness he was unable to recognize his antagonist. They wrestled until daybreak. Finally the *man,* seeing that he did not prevail over Jacob, in a sense *fouled* him. He touched his thigh so that it went out of joint, leaving him helpless.

By this time Jacob realized that he was not wrestling with a mere man but with God himself. Since he was in bodily form, we can say that his antagonist was the Son of God himself. Though physically helpless, Jacob still clung to his antagonist. Here the event takes on a spiritual tone, for Jacob holds on and pleads for a blessing. The Lord had won!

God still works in the untoward events of our lives to bring us to himself. When we realize our own helplessness, we turn to him for his blessing. What happened to Jacob has happened to many who, bereft of self-sufficiency, turn to the Lord in repentance and faith.

The blessing of the Lord was to give Jacob a new name. The supplanter became *Israel.* Several meanings have been suggested for this new name. It actually means "God strives," but in the context the name probably means "one who has prevailed with God." The name has come to mean "prince of God." The heavenly antagonist said, "For as a prince hast thou power with God and with men, and hast prevailed" (32:28). Jacob had prevailed over men with his cunning, but he had prevailed with God by submission.

Jacob lost the battle but won the war. Among the ancients a man's name represented the man; so Jacob was now a man whom God could use. No man is ready to be used of God until he forsakes self. No longer does Jacob rely upon himself, but he follows the will of the Lord.

When Esau arrived, the scene was quite different from that expected by the patriarch. As the Lord had changed Jacob so he had changed his brother. Rather than trying to kill Jacob, Esau "embraced him, and fell on his neck, and kissed him: and they wept" (33:4). It was a happy if tearful reunion of the brothers who had been sorely at odds with each other.

When Esau asked the meaning of the "drove which I met" (33:8), Jacob told him they were his gift that he "might find grace [favor, rsv] in the sight of my lord." Note "my lord" again. Only after some insistence did Esau accept the gift. Note Jacob's words: "I have seen thy face, as though I had seen the face of God, and thou wast pleased with me" (33:10). He saw forgiveness in his brother's face.

What a difference forgiveness makes where family members have been estranged! Or other parties, for that matter. When Jacob got right with God, he got right with his fellowman. This is the true essence of reconciliation.

Esau offered to travel with Jacob and his company, but Jacob protested that his group would only slow down his brother's group. When Esau suggested that he then be permitted to leave some of his men for Jacob's protection, Jacob politely refused. Instead he said, "What needeth it? let me find grace in the sight of my lord" (33:15). It should be noted that Jacob promised to meet Esau at Seir (33:14). Some see this as a lie, that he never intended to go there. If so, it was the old Jacob's nature rising to the surface again. On the other hand he may have intended going there, but later changed his plans. One would like to think that the latter is true.

At any rate it is evident that at long last Jacob became Israel, one whom God could use. The Lord had waited a long time, but time is of no consequence with him. At this point, each of us should ask if God is still waiting on us. Inevitably each must choose for or against God, and the Spirit of God ever strives with us to surrender to the Lord's will. How wonderful it would be if we would hold on to him until he blesses us as he did Israel!

The remainder of the story that centers in Jacob is brief. From Penuel he went to Succoth where he built him a house and booths for his cattle. It seems that he was thinking of settling down (33:17). Later he removed to Shechem. There he bought a piece of land which probably is the site of Jacob's well, a mecca for tourists today.

Commitment

But while Jacob was a changed man, he was not yet a committed man. The remainder of the story regards his *commitment*. This took place at Bethel where he had had a signal experience more than twenty years previously, though some say that it was thirty years later.

God said, "Arise, go up to Bethel . . . and make there an altar unto God" (35:1). That Jacob was progressing in his spiritual life is seen in his order to his entire household to put away their strange gods and idolatrous ornaments, no doubt including the household gods which Rachel had taken. Such should not be allowed to pollute so sacred a place as Bethel, the house of God. Jacob buried them under the oak (terebinth) tree; then he and his group ascended to Bethel.

There he built an altar, calling the place "El-beth-el" (35:7), the God of the house of God. Once again God repeated the promises to Jacob which he had made to Abraham and Isaac (35:11–12), after having repeated his change in name from Jacob to Israel (35:10). Jacob's earlier experience at Bethel had been a personal one, but now his family is included as they learn the meaning of this sacred place.

Jacob's return to Bethel marked the beginning of a new phase in his life. He had been changed at Penuel, but now he was committed to God's promises which involved his redemptive purpose. It is one thing to be a changed man, to become a Christian; it is a further step in one's spiritual pilgrimage to become dedicated to God and his purpose. In a very definite sense Jacob had truly become Israel (35:21).

However, this high experience was soon followed by the saddest hour in Jacob's life. As he journeyed southward from Bethel toward Hebron, Rachel died in childbirth. Tradition says that this happened near Bethlehem. Her tomb is said to be just outside this town.

Before she died, Rachel named her son Benoni, "son of my sorrow," but later Jacob named him Benjamin, "son of my right hand." The right hand is said to be the position of honor. Subsequent events reveal that of all Jacob's sons Joseph and Benjamin were his favorites, which testifies to his great love for Rachel.

One's commitment to God's purpose does not insulate him from sorrow, but God uses it to mature his children, if they trust in him. It is not what happens to one, but how he takes it that counts.

Note that in Genesis 35:21 the writer says that *Israel* journeyed. Hereafter many times he will be referred to as Jacob, but it is significant that the name Israel is used here. He was now fully a man whom God could use in carrying forward the divine promises and purpose.

Later Jacob came to Hebron where his aged father still lived, but soon thereafter Isaac died. He was buried by Jacob and Esau in Hebron in the burial place for Abraham, Sarah, and Rebekah. As Ishmael and Isaac had earlier been brought together in their father's death, so it was with Esau and Jacob. Jacob continues to appear in the Genesis story, but from here on the central character is Joseph.

It is worthy of note that God permitted Isaac to live long after he thought his death was near. Why? Was it not due to the fact that he must prepare Jacob so that he would become the proper character through whom Abraham's *seed* should run? The line must not be broken. As soon as Jacob truly became Israel, God released Isaac from the burden of old age.

Down the ages the line has run. The *seed* found fulfillment in Christ, and those who believe in him are the true seed of Abraham (Gal. 3:29). Through the centuries, even today, the shadow and light appear, but always God works through those who, despite their human weaknesses, by his grace become fit instruments of his will. Christ is the true ladder from earth to heaven (John 1:51), and all who believe in him, not only ascend the ladder, but through faithful service show the way to others who amidst the shadow reach up after him who is the Light of the world.

Weak though we are, we find strength in him who never fails. In this conviction we struggle on. Though men may stumble and fall, he is ever the same. And the glad truth is that every son of Jacob may in Christ become a son of Israel.

It fortifies my soul to know
That though I perish, Truth is so:
That, howsoe'er I stray and range,
Whate'er I do, Thou dost not change.
I steadier step when I recall
That, if I slip, Thou dost not fall.
                —Arthur Hugh Clough

10

JOSEPH: THE SLAVE WHO BECAME A SAVIOR

Genesis 37; 39–50

THIS FINAL SECTION of Genesis relates the life of Joseph, about whom the Bible gives more personal details than any other of its characters. It tells how Israel came to be in Egypt and subsequently in slavery, where the family of Jacob became a great people through whom Jehovah proposed to carry forward his redemptive purpose. Furthermore, the narrative foreshadows the redeeming work of God's Son. As God's beloved Son, Christ descended to the position of a slave only to be highly exalted by his Father, and in the process he provided salvation for all who come to him in faith. In him God worked amid men's evil to provide life. Furthermore, the Son offers forgiveness to those who sin against him. These things which are infinitely in Christ are found finitely in Joseph.

Treachery

The first part of Joseph's life may be summed up in the word *treachery*. The treachery came to him from members of his own family. Like Jesus, "he came unto his own, and his own received him not" (John 1:11).

As the story opens, Joseph is seventeen years old and estranged from his older half-brothers. To begin with, he was the firstborn of Rachel's sons; they were sons of Leah or of Jacob's two concubines. Then Joseph was a talebearer, reporting to his father on the evil doing of his brothers. Also, forgetting the tragedy of parental favoritism in his own life, Jacob loved Joseph more than his other children (Gen. 37:3–4). He made him a "coat of many colours." The description of this coat may be better rendered "a long robe with sleeves," which would imply that Joseph was not required to do manual labor, since those doing it wore sleeveless tunics. Furthermore, such a robe, later worn by royalty (2 Sam. 13:18), signified that Jacob had chosen him to succeed as head of the entire tribe or family. Normally this position would have fallen to Reuben, Jacob's firstborn by Leah, but Reuben had had sinful relations with Bilhah, his father's concubine (Gen. 35:22). Jacob later said that by that act Reuben forfeited his rights as the firstborn (49:3–4). The other brothers resented this change which was evidenced by Joseph's coat. "They hated him, and could not speak peaceably unto him" (37:4).

It is evident also that Joseph entertained ideas of grandeur for himself. On one occasion he had two dreams which he insisted on telling his brothers. Perhaps in his naïve youth he gave no forethought to their reactions, but his impertinence also suggests his state of mind in his relationships with his brothers.

In one dream he and his brothers were working in the grain harvest. His sheaf stood upright, and theirs bowed down before it. His brothers' response to the dream was "Shalt thou indeed reign . . . have dominion over us?" (37:8). This only added to their hatred. In the other dream, Joseph said that the sun, moon, and eleven stars made obeisance to him. To the brothers and even to Jacob this suggested that not only would his eleven brothers become subservient to him, but that Joseph would also be over his father and mother (Leah? or even his already dead mother Rachel?). Even Jacob rebuked him for this (37:9–10).

While these dreams were partly psychological in nature, subsequent events proved that they were prophetic. Joseph's brothers probably caught the point, for they envied or were jealous of him, but Jacob "observed the saying" or "kept the saying in mind" (RSV). This reminds us of Mary pondering in her heart things related to the birth of Jesus (Luke 2:19).

The hatred of Joseph's brothers came to a head when his father sent him to inquire of their welfare (Gen. 37:12 ff.). While Joseph stayed at home, they had taken the flocks and herds from the scanty fields about Hebron to the lush grazing land in the area of Shechem. This was quite a distance from Hebron, and they had probably been away for several months. Joseph finally found them at Dothan, about fifteen miles north of Shechem.

In this area you can see a long distance; so while Joseph was quite a way from them, the brothers saw him coming. Probably they recognized him at this distance because he wore his long robe (37:23). The robe itself inflamed their animosity against him. Why would he wear such a robe on a long journey? It can be seen only as Joseph's pride in his superior position. Due to past experience the brothers probably surmised that Joseph had come to spy on them and report to his father.

"Behold, this dreamer [Hebrew, "master of dreams," spoken in contempt] cometh" (37:19). They agreed to kill him while he was away from the protection of his doting father. They would say that a wild beast devoured him, and that would put an end to his hated dreams!

To Reuben's credit, whom Joseph was to replace in the birthright, he refused to be a party to his brother's murder. Cleverly he suggested that they put him in a pit or dry water cistern, presumably to die of hunger and thirst. Actually, he hoped that their rage would cool or that he could secretly rescue the lad and return him to his father.

Agreeing, the brothers seized Joseph, stripped him of his precious coat, and placed him in a dry cistern (37:23–24). These cisterns were tapered to a small opening at the top so that it was impossible for one to climb out unassisted. Doubtless Joseph kept crying out for help, but rather than helping him, "they sat down to eat bread" (37:25). This shows how calloused they were.

Later, confessing their crime they said, "We are truly guilty concerning our brother, in that we saw the anguish of his soul, when he besought us, and we would not hear" (42:21). This may refer to the moment when they put him in the pit, but it may also infer their indifference to his cries from the pit.

Barnhouse (vol. 2, p. 161) makes a telling comment. "A physicist could compute the exact time required for his cries to go twenty-five yards to the eardrums of the brothers. But it took twenty-five years for that cry to go from their eardrums to their hearts."

Before condemning these brothers, we should ask how deaf we are to the cries of a hurting and sinful world. How far is it from our eardrums to our hearts? Jesus was ever responsive to the needs of men, but, alas, how cold and hard are our hearts as we sit down to *eat bread* amid the pleas of the hungry, needy, and sinful!

While they were eating, the brothers, with Reuben absent, saw a trade caravan of Ishmeelites (Ishmaelites) approaching (37:25). This was on a trade route to Egypt. Judah seized the opportunity to propose that instead of killing Joseph or letting him die in the cistern, they sell him to these traders. Why not make a profit out of their crime? The rest agreed. In the meantime a band of Midianite merchantmen happened to come near the cistern which was probably some distance from the brothers. Hearing Joseph's cries, they drew him out of the cistern, and later sold him to the Ishmaelites who took him to Egypt (37:28). This raises a question, since later he is said to have been sold in Egypt by the Midianites (37:36). Some see the Ishmaelites and Midianites as the same people. Others see a mixed caravan of both. In any case the brothers seem not to have gained a profit out of it. Joseph was stolen out of the land of the Hebrews (40:15). His charge that his brothers sold him into Egypt (45:4) is Joseph's own view of the matter. At any rate their treacherous deed brought about the result.

This phase of the Joseph story has several lessons for us. To make one child in the family a pet invites trouble with the others. Even though Joseph had fallen upon good fortune in the family relationship, he should not have flaunted it before his less fortunate brothers. Furthermore, we should guard our hearts against envy, for it is a short step from envy to hate. If we harbor ill will toward others, who can predict the end toward which it will drive us?

When Reuben returned, he went to the cistern and found it empty. Nothing was said to him about the plot to sell Joseph. The fact is that none of the brothers actually knew what had happened to him. Reuben's discovery threw him into deep mourning as seen in the Oriental custom of tearing one's clothes (37:29). But whatever the outcome, all of the brothers were involved; so they decided upon a strategy to clear their skirts with their father.

Killing a small goat, they dipped Joseph's coat in its blood (37:31). When they returned home, they showed the coat to Jacob, pretending to have found it. The desired impression was that they had not seen Joseph. They pretended not to know whether the coat was Joseph's or not—as if they could ever forget the hated garment! Note that they said "thy son's," not "our brother's."

Of course, the father recognized the coat as Joseph's. He assumed the worst—that Joseph had been devoured by some wild beast, many of which roamed the area at that time. The brothers never said what may have happened to Joseph. Even if they suspected, they did not tell. One thing they did know—the blood on the coat was not Joseph's! Jacob, who had tricked so many, was now tricked by his sons. God forgives sin, but he does not always remove its consequences.

Jacob went into deep mourning (37:34). The attempted comfort of his children was to no avail. It is difficult to see the efforts of his sons as sincere. They spoke words, but only to hide their treachery rather than to console their grief-stricken father, who would mourn the rest of his life—so he thought.

Oh, the grief that has been caused by man's inhumanity to man! The tears that have flowed, the hearts that have been broken as evil men vent their envy and hatred on each other! What happened within this one family is but one aspect of the misery of the human family, because men love self and things more than God or other men. Future events reveal that God overruled the evil deeds of Joseph's brothers to work out one phase of his redemptive purpose, but this does not minimize their guilt. Likewise, God's overruling the betrayal and crucifixion of his Son does not lessen the guilt of those who did it. Truly God works in all things for good to those who love him and who fit themselves in his benevolent will (Rom. 8:28).

Testing

Genesis 39–40 relates the *testing* through which Joseph went in Egypt. He was sold as a slave to "Potiphar, an officer of Pharaoh, captain of the guard" (39:1). *Potiphar* means "he whom the sun god Ra has given." His position as a court official was, literally, "chief of the executioners," or Pharaoh's bodyguard. It should be noted that *Pharaoh* was not a personal name but a title, like *President*.

The first test to which Joseph was subjected was his state of servitude. He who had dreams of grandeur was now a slave. How would he react? Apparently he accepted it with all grace. Without complaint he went about his duties, and Jehovah was with him in all that he did. "He was a prosperous [successful, RSV] man" (39:2). Noting this fact, Potiphar made him the *overseer* of his house. He was over other slaves and controlled everything his master owned. So completely did Potiphar trust Joseph that he concerned himself only with the food he ate. The fact that God prospered Joseph meant that prosperity spread throughout his master's house.

Already we can see the hand of Jehovah directing events

toward his own purpose. Joseph had risen above the other slaves to become an important person in the household of a prominent court official. While we cannot always understand what happens to us, if we trust in the Lord, he will direct our paths in his way. God is the God of history, and while he does not perpetrate men's evil deeds, he works in the circumstances to guide history toward his intended redemptive goal.

Moses points out that Joseph was "a goodly person, and well favoured" (39:6). The Revised Standard Version more aptly renders this "handsome and good-looking." This fact brought about Joseph's second test.

Potiphar's wife sought to seduce Joseph (39:7). After all, was he not a slave who should do her bidding? Why should a slave care about morality? He was but property in a strange land. Apart from the physical aspect involved, Joseph's ego was tempted. It would be quite a prize for a slave to be intimate with one of such high standing. Everything in the situation tended toward pulling Joseph down—except his integrity of character and his faith in Jehovah. Evidently his father had proved to be a *prince with God* in instilling these qualities in his favorite son.

During the tender years of childhood, parents may control a child's actions simply by saying, "Do this" or "Don't do that." But there comes the time when a young man or woman is on his/her own. Happy is that one whose parents have planted and nourished the quality of character and a faith in God which enable him to make the right choice for himself. Joseph was such a fortunate person. His refusal to be seduced is a classic.

"Behold, my master wotteth [knoweth] not what is with me in the house, and he hath committed all that he hath to my hand; There is none greater in this house than I; neither hath he kept back any thing from me but thee, because thou art his wife: how then can I do this great wickedness, and sin against God?" (39:8-9).

Joseph refused to betray his master's trust or to befoul his wife.

Even if his "situation ethics" allowed him to do otherwise, he would not sin against God, for this would be the greatest sin of all (see Ps. 51:4).

Potiphar's sensuous wife was persistent. Day after day she offered herself to him, but always he refused. His refusal "to be with her" (Gen. 39:10) suggests that he avoided her when he could. However, his household duties made this altogether impossible. Finally on an occasion as he went about his work, and when no other slaves were in the house, she sought to force the issue. In so doing she caught him by his garment (39:12). Joseph did the only wise thing under the circumstance—he ran from the house—but he left his garment behind in this wicked woman's grasp.

"Hell hath no fury like a woman scorned"—and she wreaked it all upon Joseph. She called in the other men slaves and accused this "Hebrew" of trying to rape her. The garment left behind was telltale evidence. Perhaps the other slaves were only too glad to believe it about another slave placed over them. Had she tried, even successfully, to seduce other slaves? If so, none came to Joseph's defense. She implied that her husband was to blame by bringing this *Hebrew* into the household. To her mock righteous indignation she added the vicious note of prejudice.

When Potiphar returned home, she faced him with the garment and the same story. "The Hebrew servant, which thou hast brought unto us" (39:17). In her story the sensuous suggestions to Joseph became a cry for help from his amorous advances. Poor little innocent lamb—she had been so shamed and mistreated! Her offer of intimacy having been rebuffed, she sought vengeance. Such an act on a slave's part normally would lead to his death. Evidently that is what she intended.

Naturally Potiphar was angered, and he put Joseph in prison, the one where the king's prisoners were placed. Potiphar's actions suggest that he suspected his wife's story. Rather than executing Joseph for his "crime," he put him in the royal prison. Was this to stop his wife's tongue and to save his face? Potiphar is called "captain of the guard" (39:1), the same title of the one who gave Joseph care over other notable prisoners (40:4). Could it be then that both of these references are to Potiphar? It would seem, therefore, that rather than putting Joseph in a common prison, Potiphar kept him in the prison of which he was in charge. This is most suggestive.

Nevertheless, Joseph was further reduced from Potiphar's steward to being a prisoner—falsely accused. Thus he was subjected to another testing. Surely he had every human reason to be bitter, but no such feeling is evident in his conduct. He went on doing his job without complaint. The secret is that Jehovah was with him (39:21) in adversity and strengthened him in his trial. Soon the keeper of the prison took note of him and placed him in charge of other prisoners to direct them in their work.

The Lord may permit his people to walk in hard places, but he walks with them. The qualities which he places in them enable them to rise above untoward circumstances as they progress toward the achievement of his will. Jesus was hated by the world and told his disciples that the world would hate them.

Joseph had still another test facing him. In many ways it was the severest of all—the trial of waiting.

Pharaoh's butler and baker offended him. How is not stated, but it probably was related to an attempt on the ruler's life. In Nehemiah 1 the same Hebrew word for "butler" is rendered "cupbearer." These were responsible positions, each having to do with the food eaten by Pharaoh. A favorite way of removing rulers was by poisoning, so trusted men were responsible for his food and drink. It may have been that Pharaoh became ill after eating and drinking and that these men were suspected of trying to poison the ruler. Therefore, both were put in prison by the captain of the guard, Potiphar. That they were put "in ward in the house of the captain of the guard" (40:3) suggests a prison connected with Potiphar's house. It was here that Joseph and the two notable prisoners were kept. In fact, Joseph was given the task of serving them.

One night both men had a dream. The next morning when Joseph went to serve them, he noticed that they were sad. When asked why, they told of their dreams and the fact that there was no one in the prison to interpret them. Had they been free, there were interpreters available in the royal court. Joseph reminded them that such interpretations belong to God and asked that they tell him their dreams (40:9–13, 16–19).

The cupbearer's dream was about three clusters of ripe grapes from which he pressed the juice into Pharaoh's cup and gave it to him. Joseph told him that this meant that in three days he would be restored to his position. The baker's dream involved three baskets on his head, the top one containing "bakemeats" for Pharaoh, but birds came and ate them. Joseph told him that within three days he would be beheaded and his body impaled. Apparently investigation showed that the baker was the guilty party. It happened as Joseph said.

Joseph requested that when the cupbearer was restored, he would bring Joseph's case to Pharaoh's attention. He related how he had become a slave in Egypt, and avowed that he had done nothing punishable by being put in prison (40:14–15). One would think that the cupbearer would have been only too glad to return the favor, but as soon as he was restored he forgot Joseph. For two long years Joseph remained in prison.

This must have been the greatest trial of all, the hardest years of his life. Day after day when someone entered the prison, Joseph's heartbeat must have grown faster in hopeful anticipation. "Maybe this is the message for my release!" But not so. Disappointment followed disappointment, until he must have concluded that he was fated to remain in prison the rest of his life.

The fact that he was innocent made his state of mind and spirit all the more susceptible to bitterness and despair, but there is no evidence that Joseph fell victim to such feelings.

It is so easy to forget past favors, and so cruel. If lack of gratitude wounds men's hearts, how much greater is the hurt to God's heart. One is never greater than when he gives thanks, even for small favors, or so base as when he accepts the goodness of others, but never gives in return.

The story is told of a man speaking critically of another. Hearing it, someone said, "I am surprised to hear you say that. I thought he had done many helpful things for you!" To which the other replied, "Yes. But he hasn't done anything lately." Such an attitude is to live even below the animal level.

Triumph

Joseph was forgotten by men but not by God, and this fact led to his ultimate *triumph*. Even though the cupbearer forgot him, God used this to his glory and for his servant's good. Had Joseph been released immediately after his request, he might have congratulated himself on shrewd foresightedness. As it turned out, he could contribute his release only to God's goodness.

Two years after the cupbearer's release from prison, Pharaoh also dreamed—in fact, twice in one night. In the one dream he saw seven fat cows come up out of the Nile River. Then seven lean ones came out of the river and ate the fat ones (Gen. 41: 2–4). Egypt depends upon the Nile for irrigation; without it, the land would be desert. In the other dream, seven fine ears of corn (grain) grew on one stalk, but they were devoured by seven thin ears (41:5–7).

Troubled by his dreams, Pharaoh called in his court magicians or sacred scribes the next morning to interpret. But they were unable to do so.

Then the cupbearer remembered Joseph (41:9 ff.). He told Pharaoh about Joseph's accurate interpretation of dreams. As a result, Joseph was ordered to appear before Pharaoh. Shaved and dressed in clean clothes, he appeared in court (41:14). As a Semite, Joseph normally wore a beard. We now know that the pharaohs of this period were clean-shaven and required all who appeared before them to be likewise. The detail about Joseph's shaving attests to the authenticity of the narrative.

When he was told to interpret the dream, Joseph again said that only God does this. He was not merely a magician but a servant of Jehovah. Upon hearing the dreams, Joseph told Pharaoh that they were actually one, or had one meaning (41:25–32). They said that Egypt would have seven years of plenty and seven years of famine. Joseph went on to advise Pharaoh to seek out a man to be in charge of storing up grain in the plentiful years to provide for the lean ones. Pharaoh liked the idea and he called his advisers together to consider the matter. "Can we find such a one as this is, a man in whom the Spirit of God is?" he asked them (41:38). This is the first biblical mention of the Holy Spirit coming upon a man, and it came from the mouth of a pagan. God at times uses strange instruments to accomplish his purposes (Isa. 44:28).

Since God through Joseph had revealed the situation and plan, he was the logical one to supervise it (Gen. 41:39 ff.). He was made the second in command under Pharaoh—the viceroy of Egypt. Only Pharaoh had greater power than Joseph. Among other things he gave Joseph his signet ring with which to seal his orders. Joseph's word was Pharaoh's word. He was arrayed in fine Egyptian linen and wore an ornamental gold chain. In processions his chariot was second only to Pharaoh's, and the people were to bow before him as he rode along.

Talk about "rags to riches"! Joseph's story was "riches to rags to riches"! One morning he awoke in prison; that night he slept in the palace. Since he was thirty years old at the time (41:46), it had been about thirteen years since he arrived in Egypt as a slave. Now he was virtually the ruler of the land! It had all been God's work. Despite men's evil, God overruled to his own purpose, which suggests that no man should ever despair of his present position. With faith in God he can rise above the circumstance to be used of the Lord for his glory.

Someone has said that God's greatest victories are won on the battlefields that have seen our biggest defeats. Charles Kingsley once said, "The men whom I have seen succeed best in life have always been cheerful and hopeful men, who went about their business with a smile on their faces, and took the changes and chances of this life like men, facing rough and smooth alike as it comes." This serves as a good description of Joseph if you add the notes of virtue and faith in God.

> Well to suffer is divine.
> Pass the watchword down the line—
>   Pass the countersign, Endure!
> Not to him who rashly dares,
> But to him who nobly bears
>   Is the Victor's garland sure.
>   —John Greenleaf Whittier

With his new charge from Pharaoh, Joseph proceeded to store up grain above the actual needs of the people (41:49, 53–57). The seven years of plenty were followed by seven years of leanness. The famine was not in Egypt alone but in surrounding nations as well. Nevertheless, through his servant, God had provided.

At this point the scene shifts to Jacob and his family in Canaan. Thus begins a series of visits by Jacob's sons to purchase grain in Egypt, which culminated in the removal of Jacob's family to Egypt (Gen. 42–46). Jehovah had told Abraham that his seed would sojourn in Egypt (15:13–16). The famine provided the occasion for the beginning of the fulfillment of Jehovah's word.

With the loss of Joseph, Jacob's favorite son was Benjamin, his other son by Rachel. But as the story unfolds, there is no evidence of resentment on the part of the other brothers. They had learned their lesson in their tragic treatment of Joseph. The University of Hard Knocks has a stern curriculum, but it teaches lasting lessons.

When Jacob sent his sons to Egypt to buy grain, he kept

Benjamin with him (42:4). When the ten brothers appeared before Joseph, he recognized them, but they did not recognize him. When they had last seen him he was seventeen years old; now he was at least thirty-seven. Also he was clean-shaven and occupied a high position in the government. This was the last place they would expect to find him. Furthermore, insofar as they knew, he was dead.

At a casual glance Joseph's treatment of his brothers may seem harsh, but careful study shows that he proposed to determine their present attitude toward their father and his full-brother. At times it may seem that God deals harshly with us, but his treatment is designed to bring us to repentance and to mold us according to his benevolent will.

Joseph began by accusing the brothers of being spies sent to determine the weakness or strength of Egypt (42:9–23). They, of course, denied it, telling of their family in Canaan. Note "the youngest is this day with our father, and one is not" (42:13). Knowing that the youngest was Benjamin, Joseph told them to send one to bring him to Egypt while the others remained in prison. Only thus could they prove that they were not spies. Then he put them in prison for three days.

On the third day Joseph, as a man who feared God, changed his demand. One brother should be kept as a hostage while the others took grain to their father. They were to return with Benjamin or else the hostage would die, and he would not receive them.

Though Joseph spoke his brothers' language, to conceal his identity he spoke to them in Egyptian through an interpreter (42:23). Thinking that he could not understand them, the brothers spoke among themselves of their treatment of Joseph. Joseph was so filled with emotion as they admitted their guilt and just punishment for it that he turned away to weep. Before one can be forgiven, he must admit his sin. Joseph had brought them to this point, even if the confession was just among themselves.

Holding Simeon as hostage, Joseph sent the others back to

Canaan with grain and provisions for the journey (42:24–38). He also had each man's purchase money placed in his sack. At their first stop, one discovered his money in the sack. For some strange reason the others did not examine theirs, but they were distressed as to what would happen to Simeon if their *theft* of the money was discovered. Arriving home they reported all that had happened to them. Emptying their sacks they found each man's money. Jacob's anguish is seen in his words, "Me have ye bereaved of my children [had Jacob come to suspect his sons' treachery concerning Joseph?]: Joseph is not, and Simeon is not [with the seeming *theft* of money he was as good as dead], and ye will take Benjamin away: all these things are against me" (42:36). Despite Reuben's pledge of the life of his two sons for Benjamin's safety, Jacob refused to let them take him to Egypt.

However, the famine grew worse (Gen. 43). The brothers refused to return to Egypt without Benjamin, for without him they could not even get an audience with the viceroy. So Jacob relented. Not only did they take gifts to the viceroy, but twice the amount of money necessary for the purchase. Thus they hoped to prove that they were not thieves (43:11–12).

When they arrived in Egypt, Joseph proposed a noon meal with them. The brothers feared treachery (the scales were now tipped in the opposite direction). Arriving at the house, they explained to Joseph's steward about the money. Perhaps at Joseph's instructions he put their mind at ease, saying, "I had your money" (43:23). The other was explained as a gift from God. In actuality, Joseph *gave* them the grain.

Their arrival in Joseph's presence is a tender scene (43:27–31). He inquired as to their father's health and seeing Benjamin, he said, "God be gracious unto thee, my son" (43:29). It was too much for Joseph. Not yet ready to reveal his identity, he left the room to weep in private. Refreshed, he returned for the meal.

When the brothers, including Simeon, prepared to return home, Joseph posed another test (Gen. 44). In addition to putting each brother's money in his sack, he had his personal silver cup placed in Benjamin's sack. Joseph wished to see how the other brothers would react to a threat to Benjamin. After their departure, Joseph sent men to overtake and accuse them of taking the cup —an action they strongly denied (44:7–11). They even agreed that if anyone had the cup he would become Joseph's slave. To the other brothers' despair, the cup was found in Benjamin's sack. When they returned to Joseph, Judah made a classic plea on his youngest brother's behalf (44:18–34). He climaxed it by offering himself as Benjamin's substitute in slavery. This plea sounds like Judah's greatest Descendant pleading for the souls of men.

Judah's plea broke Joseph's heart. He now knew how changed his formerly treacherous brothers were. They cared not only for their father but for Benjamin as well. The once disrupted family was now one—with one exception. To them Joseph was dead.

So clearing the room of all but his brothers, Joseph revealed to them his identity (Gen. 45). Weeping so loudly as to be heard throughout the palace, he said, "I am Joseph!" Naturally the brothers were troubled. Would they now be punished for their foul deed many years before? Joseph allayed their fears. While they actually had sold (or caused to be sold) him into Egypt, "God did send me before you to preserve life" (45:3–5). Rather than taking vengeance upon them, he saw God's purpose in it all. All that had happened to him had not been God's doing, for God does not work evil. But he had overruled the evil to work good.

Joseph did not use his position of power to "get even" for past wrongs. Rather he showed compassion and forgiveness to the helpless and repentant. In this he demonstrated his godlike character. Truly, as Alexander Pope said, if it is human to err, it is divine to forgive.

The remainder of the story of Genesis is concerned with Joseph's bringing his father's family to Egypt and settling them in the land of Goshen, an area designed as a perfect place for grazing herds and flocks. At long last Jacob's family is *united*.

Jacob died in peace after having blessed his sons. He was buried in Canaan in the cave of Machpelah (50:13).

The most important blessing was given to Judah. Eventually his tribe emerged as the ruling one (King David was of the tribe of Judah). But Jacob looked beyond David to "the Son" of David. "The sceptre shall not depart from Judah . . . until Shiloh come; and unto him shall the gathering of the people be" (49:10). The meaning of *Shiloh* is vague. The most likely one is "to whom it belongs"—or the right to use the sceptre. This is usually referred to the Messiah; so here is the first definite messianic promise.

Joseph finally died at the age of one hundred and ten, a ripe age among the Egyptians (50:22). Before his death he requested that when Israel returned to Canaan after the exodus, they would take his mummified body and bury it in the land of promise (50:24–25; Heb. 11:22). He believed in the promise Jehovah made to Abraham. At the time of the exodus (Exod. 13:19) the Israelites took his body and later buried it in Shechem (Josh. 24:32).

Thus Genesis, which opens with the bright light of creation, closes with the words "a coffin in Egypt." Were it not for the rest of the Bible, it would be a dismal ending, but Joseph's request makes it a symbol of faith. Through their long years of servitude, the Israelites could find in that coffin a ground for hope. It was as a light of faith shining in the darkness of despair. Francisco (p. 52) expresses it in succinct terms. "In Genesis 1:1 God created light. In Genesis 50:25–26 Joseph turned his face toward it."

Joseph, who went from "riches to rags to riches," looked forward to "Shiloh" whom his life finitely typifies.

"Who, being in the form of God, thought it not robbery [something to be grasped and held on to] to be equal with God: But made himself of no reputation [emptied himself], and took upon him the form of a servant, and was made in the likeness of men: And being found in fashion as a man, he humbled himself, and became obedient unto death, even the death of the cross. Wherefore God also hath highly exalted him, and given him a name which is above every name: That at the name of Jesus every knee should bow . . . And that every tongue should confess that Jesus Christ is Lord, to the glory of God the Father" (Phil. 2:6–11).

Let us then look beyond the coffin in Egypt to the empty tomb, yea, to the occupied throne, to the Lord's return—even to him who, though rich, became poor that we might as children of God become heirs of God and joint-heirs with him.

BIBLIOGRAPHY

Atkinson, Basil F. C. *Pocket Commentary on the Bible*. Chicago: Moody Press, 1957.

Barnhouse, Donald Grey. *Genesis, Vols. 1, 2*. Grand Rapids, Mich.: Zondervan, 1970.

Bright, John. In *The Biblical Archaeologist* 5 (Dec. 1942): 55–62.

Davies, G. Henton. *Broadman Bible Commentary, Vol. 1*. Nashville: Broadman, 1969.

Driver, S. R. *The Book of Genesis: Westminster Commentaries*. London: Methuen & Co., 1904.

Fairbairn, Andrew M. *The Philosophy of the Christian Religion*. New York: Macmillan, 1902.

Filby, Frederick A. *The Flood Reconsidered*. Grand Rapids, Mich.: Zondervan, 1971.

Francisco, Clyde. *Teacher's Bible Commentary*. Nashville: Broadman, 1972.

Pfeiffer, Charles F. *Book of Genesis*. Grand Rapids, Mich.: Baker, 1958.

Thielicke, Helmut. *How the World Began*. Philadelphia: Muhlenberg Press, 1961.

Watts, J. W. *A Distinctive Translation of Genesis*. Grand Rapids, Mich.: Eerdmans, 1963.